IN SEARCH OF

THE
MOUNTAIN
OF GOD

IN SEARCH OF

THE
MOUNTAIN
OF GOD

THE DISCOVERY OF THE REAL MT. SINAI

ROBERT CORNUKE
AND
DAVID HALBROOK

BROADMAN
&HOLMAN
PUBLISHERS

Nashville, Tennessee

0–8054–2052–5

Published by Broadman & Holman Publishers, Nashville, Tennessee

Dewey Decimal Classification: 221
Subject Heading: BIBLE

Scripture quotations are from the Holy Bible, New International
Version, © copyright 1973, 1978, 1984
by the International Bible Society.

Library of Congress Cataloging-in-Publication Data

Cornuke, Bob, 1951–
   In search of the moutain of God : the discovery of the real Mt.
Sinai / Bob Cornuke and David Halbrook.
      p. cm.
   ISBN 0-8054-2052-5 (hc)
   1. O.T. Exodus—Geography. 2. Arabian Peninsula in the Bible.
3. Revelation on Sinai. 4. Sinai, Mount (Egypt) 5. O.T.—Evidence,
authority, etc. I. Halbrook, David. II. Title.

BS630.C67 2000
221.9'1—dc21

                                                      00–023639

3 4 5 04 03 02 01 00

Contents

Acknowledgments

Time is cruel to those seeking clues to our past, and researching ancient mysteries of the Bible can be especially so. With every day, year, decade, and century that passes, the trail of truth becomes fainter and fainter. It requires a special grit and stubborn determination to forge ahead (often against the grain of accepted scholarship and public opinion), to find the elusive, faded shreds of clues cloaked within the ever-darkening veil of history. These hard journeys across vast frontiers of time and distance are often dangerous, filled with hardship, fraught with controversy, and would be impossible without the help of some very special people.

It is difficult to adequately convey appropriate appreciation to so many who generously assisted in this literary and research effort. I would like to specifically mention my wife Terry, who provided endless support and encouragement through years of travel and ministry, and my family Paul, Brandon,

Mandy, Michelle, Nancy, John, Connor, Shannon, and Mom for standing by me as I ventured into unknown worlds with unfamiliar rules. I would like to thank Larry Williams for his courage and vision; Jim and Penny Caldwell for risking their lives for the sake of research in Saudi Arabia; Dr. Roy Knuteson for his groundbreaking theories on the Exodus route; Jim Irwin, Mary Irwin, Sig Swanstrom, Mike Barnes, Ray and Carole Ardizzone for their godly example and friendship; David Halbrook for being a very special friend and gifted writer; and Steve Halliday for his thoughtful editing touch. Above all I give the praise and glory to my Lord and Savior for revealing more to me through his Word than all the libraries in the world.

Bob Cornuke

Introduction

AN UNPARALLELED ADVENTURE

Its crest can be seen from quite a distance—it is, after all, the tallest mountain in the region. The first thing one notices upon approaching Jabal al Lawz is its mysteriously blackened, startlingly visible, peak. It gives the appearance of summit shrouded in shadow—yet, oddly so, because the sky above remains ever clear and cloudless. It stands statuesque above a broad desert plateau, a mystifying relic of antiquity in a land the Bible calls Midian. And it is girdled about with barbed wire and posted with warnings by the Saudi minister of antiquities: "No Trespassing Allowed. Violators Will Be Put to Death."

Some believe troves of gold and jewels looted in Egypt by the Israelites lie buried in its bowels. But we sought, and found, treasures of another sort on its craggy slopes: a mind-boggling array of ancient, man-made structures and tantalizing geologic formations that come at one as from the pages of holy Scripture. And while we knew of others who had risked their lives to find it, Jabal al Lawz remains so veiled by time, terrain, and bogus tradition that scarcely a handful of serious scholars even know it exists. Larry Williams and I were by all accounts the only westerners to get in—and get out— with evidence. In so doing we scaled heights and shared dreams we never knew existed.

To behold the otherworldly composition of Jabal al Lawz is to be instantly spellbound, humbled, dismayed. I can never forget running a nervous hand over its slick-black crown, marveling at its glazed, ebony surface, breaking off a chunk and finding brown granite on the inside, obsidian black outside, and thinking, *What could cause that?* As we combed the mountainside with our infrared scopes and binoculars and saw its boulder-piled altars, ghostly stone pillars, and hand-cut markers and shrines scattered about the peak like road signs, we couldn't help but wonder: *Were these the puzzle pieces of a sacred mosaic?*

The evidence continued to mount up, surpassing our wildest fantasies and finally melding into an undeniable picture: Jabal al Lawz—brazen, black-crested, coy, and defiant in the land of Mecca—is . . . has to be . . . the real Mount Sinai. We had found the holy jewel of ancient Judaism, ground zero of Judeo-Christian civilization! And we have the pictures, rock samples, and testimony to prove it.

This book chronicles our life-changing adventure and invites you to decide whether our controversial conclusion stands up to inspection. In Part One you'll read of our exciting search for the real Mount Sinai; think of it as the main feature. Part Two is the "prequel" to our Arabian adventure and tells how an unsuccessful search for the chariot wheels of Pharaoh's army— sunk in the Red Sea when Israel fled slavery in Egypt thirty-five hundred years ago—led us to an even greater challenge. Part Two also builds a strong case for the reliability of the Bible in matters historical (and therefore in matters both personal and spiritual).

I hope the events detailed in this simple account lead you, as they did me, to a profound trust in the Lord of glory, the One who set Sinai aflame with his infinite majesty and power. Who could have guessed that a shabby lust for adventure would lead to the greatest discovery of all: the certain knowledge that this great God loves each one of us, personally?

Enjoy!

3

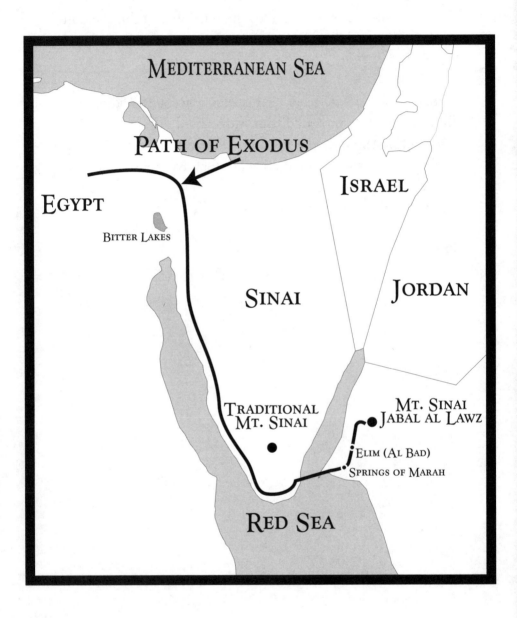

Part One

THE SEARCH FOR MOUNT SINAI

O п e

FAR FROM HOME

Heat rising from the desert floor made the interior of the concrete cell feel like a firing kiln. A rusted steel roof, scarcely high enough to stand beneath, magnified the effect, raising welts on my sunburned skin. It was the kind of scorcher one encounters only in Arabia, a wasteland far hotter than any equatorial expanse on earth.

And the smell! A stench of putrefied mutton blanketed the countryside. Centuries of sheep grazing had produced a pungent, bedrock odor that seemed to ooze from the soil itself. It vented from clothes, tent flaps, even the pores of our jailers' flesh. In our cramped cell it hung so heavy I thought I might pass out (and might have retched, but for fear of losing face before my captors). I fought the nausea, coaxing myself: *Breathe deep . . . slow and rhythmic. Stay alert! Don't lose it.*

A chattering band of leather-skinned Bedouins heckled us at gunpoint and spewed profanities in Arabic. They appeared cooly at ease in the crushing heat, even under bushy beards and dense linen fatigues—uncomplicated desert folk whiling away another lazy day in Midian. Tourists to the Middle East recognize Bedouins by their colorful garb, gaudy handmade trinkets, and cheap camel rides. But this bunch was the real deal—Masters of the Desert, as they're portrayed in literature—hardened through centuries of sun and sand.

I'd read enough to know that nomadic Saudi Bedouins enjoy a reputation as fierce warriors, quick to lay down their lives for comrades, kinsmen, and, above all, the honor of Allah. And these simple country riflemen had been deputized as Saudi military police, Frontier Forces division—a nimble, hardscrabble tribe skilled in desert reconnaissance and guerrilla warfare. Their job, from all appearances, was to patrol the interminable badlands known as the Saudi frontier, an ocean of sand, ravines, and bleak, rocky bluffs stretching from Riyadh in the east to the Red Sea in the west. This lonely regiment had charge over a territory stretching from the settlement of Al Bad in Saudi Arabia's northwestern panhandle to somewhere near the Jordanian border, a territory riddled both with highly restricted military installations and forbidden, politically explosive archaeological sites. The latter features a host of breathtaking landmarks—many straight from the Book of Exodus—and includes one particularly curious mountain known as Jabal al Lawz. The locals call it Jabal Musa, or Mountain of Moses. It was this mountain that drew us to Saudi Arabia, and, indirectly, to this squalid jail cell.

Two feet away sat my friend and traveling companion, Larry Williams. Slumped against a wall and looking disconsolate,

Larry nursed a mild case of sunstroke. We'd been sitting cross-legged on the dirt floor of the hutch for thirteen hours, trying to stay awake as the Bedouins grilled us with a flood of unintelligible questions. The torrent of Arabic numbed our brains and muddied our concentration, stifling any thought of a heroic escape. I guess they figured we were stupid enough to make a suicide dash into the desert, because they'd taken our shoes and socks and sat us down on a mat of greasy carpet crawling with red ants, which were now stinging, biting, and swarming under our shirt collars, pant legs, even underwear. We suffered silently, loath to draw unwanted attention by scratching or squirming.

The guardhouse commander barked an order, and across the room two young boys hopped up and scampered to a smoky fire pit. Across the room, a young boy hopped up and scampered to a large silver teapot. He carefully disbursed a brackish, syrupy liquid into two dainty cups. The Bedouins call it tea, but it tasted more like the rancid dregs of a vinegar vat. "Here we go again," Larry moaned. "Cheers!"

It was a drill we knew well. For the past thirteen hours, at precise fifteen-minute intervals, they had plied us with cups of this "tea." Each time we were politely *encouraged* to drink the wretched, black-green brew, which to this day ranks as the most vile liquid ever to pass my lips. But we played along with this odd, almost surreal "welcoming ceremony." Its practiced formality suggested it was conducted with the same deferential smiles and feigned cordiality, whether one was a royal guest or an enemy spy. So it went. Every quarter hour the screaming and taunting ceased so we could participate in this somber tea party.

Almost as much as the tea, I was starting to hate the crumbling guardhouse, with its sooty, foot-thick walls. I craned my neck to squint through a crack in the mortar—beyond our hovel sat the fire-baked wilderness, stretching forever into an ashen dusk. My heart sank again. Even if we managed to escape—in this heat, without water, already weakened and dehydrated—we'd be dead in three hours. To my weary gaze the landscape seemed to pitch and blur, a nightmarish vision bordering on hallucination. But from where I sat, I knew it was no hallucination. At that moment it seemed a perfect vision of hell.

CAUGHT IN THE ACT

Back in my years as a SWAT-team policeman, I'd grown used to the idea that one day, *someday*, I'd more than likely die violently—a "tacit acceptance of a quantified risk," as our police psychologists used to say. But even so, I didn't relish the idea of being held as a spy in Saudi Arabia, a country that imprisons those who dare mispronounce the name of the Prophet Mohammed. What grim sentence awaited two Americans traveling on forged visas, found with cameras in the vicinity of a secret military compound, crossing a plain rich in forbidden archaeological treasures? It couldn't be good, and the evidence against us made for an open-and-shut case.

If only we hadn't gotten disoriented in the desert and asked that passing Bedouin to point us toward an asphalt road! For all we knew, he brought us to this forsaken outpost as an act of mercy, hoping to spare us another six hours of driving in circles. For all we knew, he was as shocked as we were when the Frontier police pulled us from our truck at gunpoint and accused us of spying. But I doubt it. To the paranoid Saudis, our fair complexions and pickup full of camping equipment was the first clue we were up to some mischief. The 35mm Nikon with the telephoto lens sitting on the front seat only cinched it. Tourism of any kind is banned in the kingdom, and cameras in the possession of foreigners loitering near restricted outposts and archaeological havens look about as innocent as Uzi-toting terrorists wandering up to the White House.

Somehow they hadn't yet searched our truck. If they had, they would've immediately uncovered our stash of infrared scopes, telephoto lenses, canisters of film, and expensive metal detection equipment, as well as the topographical maps and other incriminating documents detailing our illegal intentions. These we'd tossed lazily under a tarp in the pickup bed and stuffed carelessly under the bench seat of the truck. That they are all known to be the stock tools of espionage—more than enough to get us convicted as spies and promptly shot or beheaded—hadn't seemed like such a big deal. Until now.

It seemed a miracle that our captors showed no interest in the truck's contents, for the most cursory probe would instantly confirm what we assumed they already suspected: we had trespassed beyond the barbed-wire barricade guarding Jabal al Lawz.

Of course, we were not spies but mere adventurers. We had zero interest in military espionage; it was the mountain *itself* that tantalized our imaginations and set us like bloodhounds chasing across seas and continents to its majestic foot. It was the *mountain*—an eight-thousand-foot peak prized by the Saudi government as a "treasure from antiquity"—that sent us scurrying across the punishing desert until our arrest.

11

Why had we risked our lives by stealing into a country closed to outsiders? *To find a mountain so obscure it had lain hidden from the world for more than two millennia.* We sought a granite monolith whose religious overtones rang so provocative, whose archaeological riches held such promise, that merely saying its name (*"Jabal al Lawz!"*) in the wrong company could get one tossed in jail. This prize had grown so illogically large in our minds that, sitting in this ant-infested guardhouse, I began to question my sanity. Had I taken leave of my senses? It appeared so—we *both* had—though it didn't seem to matter much now. Any minute one of these trigger-happy thugs would snatch a peek in our truck, and the charade would end.

THE DREADED TEA RITE

The guards worked themselves into a righteous rage. Their threats, infused with hateful bravado, reached an awful crescendo. The commander seemed eager to shoot us and be done with it, but something held him back. His men—laughing, mocking—slid shells into vintage flintlocks and pressed the loaded muzzles to our heads.

Through it all, I kept an eye on the young lads. Even in the uproar, they served us tea. Bless their hearts, they found some simple joy in dutifully retrieving our cups, rinsing them in the communal basin, tipping the pot, and refilling the cups. I imagined it was all some diabolic Muslim torture—the dreaded *tea rite*—known to break a man's will and hasten his confession. Had either of us spoken Arabic, we might have gone ahead and confessed rather than drink another loathsome drop.

I handed my cup to the boy, a handsome, willowy youth, about the same age as my own son, Brandon. His blousy Bedouin robe swallowed his gaunt frame, and the rusty long rifle slung over his shoulder seemed almost as tall as he. He held it proudly, a warrior's prop belying boyish innocence. His bright, eager eyes reminded me of Brandon—the same look of forced maturity I saw in his eyes as I boarded our plane in Colorado Springs two weeks earlier. The resemblance filled me with sorrow.

I rocked back, exhausted, against the wall of the clay hutch, gummy with soldier sweat and rifle grease. I closed my eyes. Had I known I'd end up here, fending off ants in a suffocating Bedouin hot box, as Arabs screamed at me from dawn to dusk, I might have stayed home. Why leave the comforts of Colorado to die here?

Then again, I might have come anyway. Larry and I knew that priceless secrets lay hidden in these jagged hills, and if this were indeed our last hurrah, then it would be a fitting end for two adventure junkies. Truth be known, it was an ending we had both envisioned.

†wo

A FRIENDSHIP FORGED

"All right," Larry Williams spluttered, his face flushed, "I *challenge* you . . ."

"To a *race?*" I asked, incredulously. "What distance?"

"A hundred yards!" he spat back.

I kept a straight face, but inside I was grinning. I knew his fondness for longer distances. "OK," I agreed, poker-faced. I pointed down a length of the shoreline. "We'll race from here to the pier."

"You got it," said Larry, stripping off his shirt.

Just moments before, Larry and I had been chatting about former athletic exploits and the struggle to stay fit. When the topic shifted to running, Larry declared that he ran marathons—and by his tone and manner he clearly thought he was pretty fast. When I replied that I had been a college running back, Larry's eyes flashed. Fairly puffing out his chest, he challenged me to a footrace. I gently begged off, cautioning him that, realistically, I'd blow his doors off. But he demanded satisfaction—*"Right here and now!"*

So we removed our sandals and took our marks in the sand. Someone called out, *"On your mark . . . Get set . . . GO!"* We exploded off the line. Or should I say, *I* exploded. Larry sort of . . . well, hurried, with great effort and form. I left him in the dust at twenty yards. Afterwards, I admitted that had the race been longer (and Larry fifteen years younger), it might have been more competitive. Larry, defiant and unbowed, informed me he'd gladly take me on again—*anytime!* (That is, *after* he'd had a chance to train for the shorter sprint.)

We both nearly died laughing, humbled at this sad case of two ex-jocks trying to recapture some shred of their former glory. And it showed me something: Larry and I were a lot alike— brash, cocky, quick with a dare, loving a challenge. A kindred spirit if I'd ever met one!

Though we are polar opposites in most respects, I found Larry Williams to be a lot of fun, the definition of a walking paradox. Larry is a world-class cynic who also happens to be thoughtful and compassionate, fiercely competent, highly intelligent, yet possessed of an impulsive temperament that spurs him to act first and weigh consequences later. On the scent of adventure, Larry freely admits that his ego causes him "to lose a bit of my rational senses."

I met Larry for the first time in 1988 as we prepared for a Red Sea expedition in which we hoped to find remnants of the Egyptian army that perished while pursuing Moses and his fleeing countrymen (see Part II). Everyone knew Larry as a

16
Λ

formidable Wall Street player, an independent commodities trader (and part-time treasure hunter) who earned a reputation for turning small stakes into million-dollar windfalls. Friends also knew him for his love of adventure and exploration, as well as his penchant for throwing money at obscure search-and-recovery projects. He loved a good caper, and after hearing the expedition's sponsor, Dick Ewing's, theories on the Exodus, Williams jumped in and bankrolled the entire Red Sea search. By the final tally, he had dropped $250,000 to cover the boat, divers, film documentary, sonar and metal detection equipment.

I wasn't sure whether to admire or pity him—but for a guy like me, who loves adventure but can rarely afford it, Larry Williams was a fellow I wanted to know. A week after our team left for Cairo, Larry flew over and met us near the Straits of Tirān. I was immediately drawn to Larry—I think it was his jesting personality and wry sense of the absurd. Understand, I'd been traveling for two weeks in a foreign country, in the close company of a few highly motivated and extremely devout men whose influence I found to be spiritually uplifting and intellectually stimulating, with one drawback: these men seemed a little stiff and somber for my taste. Then suddenly Larry shows up, with his large personality and laid-back attitude. The next thing I know, I'm having the time of my life.

For his part, Larry never pretended to have deep passion for the mission's spiritual objective. He took a mild interest in the Bible, but his thing was the *adventure*, pure and simple. He enjoyed the hunt, the thrill of discovery. He appreciated me for nothing more than that I wasn't endlessly quoting Scripture or dropping to a knee to pray at every turn. He pulled me aside once to complain about our team, in his view "a bunch of religious fanatics"—awkward territory for Larry, who tended to see Christians as finger-wagging cranks. The spiritual banter of the group set him on edge, especially when directed none-too-subtly at him—he detected a conspiracy to get him "saved." With Larry such tactics always backfired and made him even more aloof.

Though I called myself a Christian in those days, my dry wit and breezy manner didn't fit the stereotype. To Larry, I was the only other "normal" guy on board—a "guy's guy" as he liked to say. And, as our footrace attested, my presence freed him to be himself and have some fun. At those prices, he *deserved* a little fun.

FILLING THE VOID

Something else intrigued me about Larry, something that took me awhile to put my finger on. Eventually I realized that while Larry is one of the richest guys I know, making money does not motivate him—not in the slightest. Once, as we waited on deck while the divers plied the waters below, I asked Larry, *Why?* Why dump a quarter-million dollars into this star-crossed venture? He shrugged as if it were a trifling matter: "It was a whim," he said, "just a whim." I must have looked puzzled, for he sat back and casually explained not only his investment strategy but also his philosophy of life. "I'm just a wild, wacky guy," he began. "I see money as an energy force; you can't hold on to energy, but you can *do* a lot of things with energy. I happen to focus this energy on adventure. Some strange, internal force makes me throw money at these crazy explorations." Then he laughed and with a wince added, "It should probably worry me, because not even people with *real* big money finance these long shots."

For Larry it was strictly the challenge, the gut thrill of beating the system, that made him a successful trader and a zealous explorer. Reared in Montana, he grew up loving the outdoors, spending his youth spelunking in caves and digging around Indian graves for arrowheads and burial relics. As a young man he tried his hand at rodeo, proving to be a gutsy (if not terribly talented) bareback bronc rider. Then, fancying himself a writer, he majored in journalism in college. When a writing career never blossomed, he shifted his energy to the stock market. "It looked like easy money," he says. After some humbling setbacks, he got serious and set his quick intellect toward a meticulous, almost scientific, study of the market. The day soon came when he discovered he knew more about predicting the market than all his tutors.

"For years," he recalls, "I sat under college professors who smoked their pipes and sat in stuffy armchairs and told me the market isn't predictable. Well, they were flat-out *wrong*." Success made him cynical toward highbrow academicians and later shaded his attitude toward the staid discipline of archaeology. He found it tantalizing that some of the century's prominent archaeological discoveries were made not by professors or trained archaeologists but by amateur treasure hunters or dumb-lucky passersby. The list is impressive:

- Jordan's ancient city of Petra, discovered in 1812 by a Swiss explorer whose brilliant strategy consisted of politely asking a Jordanian Bedouin to take him to the fabled city.

19

- The sunken Spanish Galleon *Atocha*, with its forty tons of gold and silver, discovered by scuba guide Mel Fisher, whose sole gifts were grit and fortitude.

- The oldest petroglyphs in America, found in the Grand Canyon by a lonely cowpoke out for a morning trot.

- Or the most amazing of all, the Dead Sea Scrolls, unearthed in the Judean desert by Bedouin shepherds searching for a stray goat.

20

Bored with making money for its own sake, Larry tried politics: twice he won Montana's Republican U.S. Senate nomination and twice lost in the general election. The setbacks left him with limitless ambition, boundless assets, and nowhere to turn. Ultimately he tried to fill the void by pouring himself into treasure hunting. With a little cash, perseverence, and luck, he figured, he, too, might one day stumble upon something so grand it would turn up in the history books. It became his calling of sorts, a cause that made him feel more fully alive while feeding an almost obsessive drive to confound the experts. Looking for the priceless relic, he declares, "is very much like working the markets. In theory, the markets can't be beaten, but I've done it most of my life." When he saw how professorial types made so many mistakes in an area as simple to research and evaluate as stocks and commodities, he says, "It made me wonder about archaeological discoveries. And sure enough, most archeological finds are made by amateur treasure hunters."

Beating the markets, then, became a necessary means to an end. "They say money can't buy happiness," he says, "but it *can* buy adventure, time, and experiences. For me, there's got to be *something* bigger than simply making money."

In the winter of 1988, Larry was just the kind of eccentric benefactor I could run with: a shoot-from-the-hip risk taker who loved adventure for its own sake. And I was his perfect foil: an analytical problem solver blessed with a healthy sense of humor, willing to bend the rules to win the prize, and highly adept in risky situations. Larry had a way of drawing my talents to the surface; I helped ground his impetuous excess. We enjoyed an edgy kind of chemistry, a potent, competitive bond powerful enough to thrust us into realms we never would have ventured alone.

And maybe shouldn't have ventured together.

THREE

"IT'S OVER THERE"

How did I get here? Cloistered in our desert
dungeon, wilting under another hail of
threats, it seemed an odd question. I *knew* how
I got here. Didn't I? I'd been victimized by an
unforeseen stream of events, each tugging me,
one rash decision at a time, to this moment of
reckoning. How could I have resisted it? How
could I have turned away from this irresistible
meeting of opportunity, timing, and adventure? I doubt I would have done anything
differently—would I?

How *did* I get here?

I breathed deeply, closed my eyes, and tried to
block out the angry inquisition swirling about
us. A memory formed, a sharp image. Yes, I
saw myself sitting on the deck of the luxury
yacht *Fantasea*, admiring the moonlit west
shore of the Straits of Tiran. Larry Williams
was there. So was my friend Jim Irwin. We
were docked in the Gulf of Aqaba, where the
eastern arm of the Red Sea curls around the

tip of the Sinai Peninsula, in a leased yacht favored by movie stars and heads of state.

It was a year earlier, winter 1988. I was a junior member of a search-and-exploration team trolling the Red Sea for the legendary remains of Pharaoh's chariots or any other iron weapons or implements we might find strewn on the sea bottom. Given that Pharaoh's entire chariot corps (well over 600 drawn from across Egypt, according to Exod. 14:7) followed the fleeing Hebrews into the sea that day, only to be swallowed up in the collapsing cataract, it was reasonable to assume some of the iron-banded wheels might still survive.

Of course, verification would be extremely difficult. Ours was a microscopic quarry scattered across the bottom of one of the deepest bodies of water on earth. Yet such a prize held unspeakable promise.

The expedition was the brainchild of two devoted Christians, Dick Ewing of Portland, Oregon, and Dr. Roy Knuteson of Fort Collins, Colorado. From the beginning of this gigantic task, both men recognized there was more at stake than the recovery of Egyptian relics. A higher calling bound them together in this strange quest.

Ewing, an explorer and documentary film producer, had authored the book *The Journey of the Iron Camels* about his motorcycle trek across the Sahara. Knuteson, a pastor and biblical scholar, had spent the past decade researching the events surrounding the Exodus. Both shared an unbending faith in the absolute accuracy of Scripture. Both were convinced the Exodus story happened exactly the way the Bible says it did.

They *knew* those chariot wheels lay somewhere at the bottom of the sea, even if in tiny chips and pieces.

Chariot fragments, however, were merely a means to a greater end. Troubled by an increasingly secular society that rejected the traditional tenets of biblical Christianity, they had come to view Pharaoh's chariots as a unique proof of biblical history. They saw this expedition as a chance to demonstrate to a skeptical world that the Exodus did, in fact, happen the way the Bible says it did. If wheels or armor dated to that famous epoch could be found, it would give teeth to the historical accuracy of Scripture.

By any measure, it was a noble endeavor—but one which presented almost insurmountable challenges. In an ocean of possibilities, a team would have to determine, almost to the meter, where the Israelites actually *crossed* the sea—and theories on this topic are nearly as far-fetched as they are numerous.

Knuteson, however, had taken his Exodus research a step further than most. He steadfastly refused to acquiesce to purely secular interpretations. After his exhaustive study of Exodus literature fell well short of pinpointing the true Red Sea crossing point, he employed a fresh tactic: he dared to examine what *Scripture* had to say. By taking a hard look at the Book of Exodus, Knuteson and Ewing systematically eliminated all known Exodus route theories, then scoured hundreds of miles of Sinai coastline until they had identified a tiny swath of beach at the Straits of Tiran—the same patch of beach that got my imagination running wild on the deck of the *Fantasea*.

I had been added to the thirteen-man crew at the last minute, thanks to an invitation from my good friend, Jim Irwin. Irwin, you might recall, was the Lunar Module pilot on the Apollo 15 mission—the eighth man to walk on the moon. I'd met Jim five years earlier in Colorado Springs, Colorado, where I was selling real estate after a career in law enforcement and where Irwin directed his High Flight Foundation. (Jim founded High Flight in 1972—the year he resigned from NASA—in response to the spiritual awakening he experienced while gazing at earth from the moon's surface. High Flight aimed to locate ancient biblical artifacts that could lend evidential support to the authenticity of Scripture.)

When we first met, Jim was busy traveling the world, a celebrity ambassador active in global politics and a frequent participant on the international peace-talk circuit. High Flight had undergone a shift in focus, launching Irwin on a series of heavily publicized trips to Mount Ararat in western Turkey, where he searched aggressively for Noah's ark.

Missing police work and aching for a little adventure, I became an instant acolyte, entranced by Jim's tales of space travel and his moon-walk experience. He was also a kind, gentle man, whose tender Christian witness ultimately sparked my own spiritual awakening. He set my heart ablaze as he spoke reverently about his search for Noah's ark.

I eventually helped Jim raise $15,000 for a trip to Turkey. He appreciated my fund-raising abilities, but was more intrigued by my police experience and weapons expertise. He sealed our friendship when he invited me along on his next trip to Mount Ararat; I guess he figured I might come in handy with a gun in war-torn Turkey, where the Kurds and Turks were locked in a bloody guerrilla warfare. I soon became his bodyguard and confidant, a role that provided me lavish travel opportunities and, more importantly, the good fortune of studying at the feet of an extraordinary human being. Without trying, I'd been introduced to an exhilarating new world of adventure.

When Jim asked me along to Egypt, I knew he had no great interest in the search for Pharaoh's chariots. He was doing Ewing and Knuteson a favor, lending his name to the project to help attract financial backing. He agreed to be the focus of their documentary chronicling the search, understanding that his presence could help trigger a media buzz in the event of an earthshaking discovery.

I came along strictly for the ride. I certainly didn't qualify as a spiritual giant, but (while I didn't let on) I held a passing interest in the mission's aim. I believed in God and had read some of the Bible. I figured if stirring up some old wagon wheels from the Exodus would aid God's cause, so much the better. I prided myself on keeping an open mind; although skeptical, I was willing to be persuaded.

Jim was the *real* reason I went. His humble bearing and deep integrity had already taught me, more than a thousand sermons, the meaning of godliness. I would have followed him anywhere. I felt as thrilled to share a cup of coffee with Jim at the corner diner as I felt honored to squire him to Russia for the 1989 Kiev Peace Talks.

I handled the luggage for our flight to Egypt, weighted down with cameras and metal detection equipment, miscellaneous diving and photographic gear. I carried the crew's bags, scuba gear, and film equipment to and from the boats and buses. Chagrined at being low man on the totem pole, I first acted aloof and indifferent to the mission. *Scouring the sea floor for obscure bits of metal—it's a big waste of time and money*, I groused. *What value could there be in this musty old Exodus story?* I had never paused to ask myself if it really happened, whether it was indeed fact, legend, or something in between. Yet as we traveled into Egypt's exotic interior, the mission's quixotic allure soon disarmed and charmed me.

Touring the Sinai Peninsula and observing the culture, taking in the smells, absorbing the vibrant hues and contours proved a potent tonic. I found myself immersed in a corner of the world where the stories I learned in Sunday school actually *happened*. The wondrously diverse landscape, redolent with mythic imagery and spiritual symbolism, brought the Bible erupting to life.

And being sequestered for sixteen hours a day with a team of bold Christian men unashamed to accept Scripture at face value sharpened my curiosity! Their startling insights provoked my imagination and infused all those Bible stories with new excitement. I found myself, quite uncharacteristically, opening the Bible to compare its passages with the appearance and *feel* of the local terrain. The Bible began speaking to me in ways I'd never imagined.

We traveled down the west Sinai coastline, venturing inland at several points to test a handful of fashionable Exodus-route theories, finally arriving near the southern tip of the peninsula. We moved quickly to our final destination: the strategic beachhead on the Straits where Knuteson and Ewing's research indicated the Israelites actually *crossed* the Red Sea. It's where our search for the chariots began in earnest.

Unfortunately, the crystal clear waters off the coast proved too deep. We never found anything. Weighed down by cumbersome metal detection equipment, the divers couldn't cover much ground. The loose sandy bottom prevented effective excavation. In hindsight, our rushed, underfunded, piecemeal effort was doomed from the start.

Disappointment filled Knuteson and Ewing, while Williams started to regret having dumped a fortune into this dry well. Still, as we prepared to leave, an odd undercurrent of excitement bristled among the team members. As I was soon to discover, the trip had yielded other fascinating fruit.

As the dive team stowed its gear below deck, I sat up with Jim and Larry. As the moon shone luminescent and spindles of starlight danced diamond sparkles off the calm waters, we got swept up in a spirited dialogue about the moment, thirty-five hundred years earlier, when these very waters parted a stone's throw from our bow. Jim, normally quiet to the point of bashfulness, became upbeat and animated. We argued the different scenarios, each of us wrestling to articulate the impossible: what must it have been like for the Israelites, rushing into the brink, terrified as a canyon of water rose above them like a mountain, then seeing it collapse on the hapless Egyptians?

A movie scene kept running through my mind: the part in *The Ten Commandments* where Charlton Heston raised his staff and, in a crude bit of pre-*Star Wars* Hollywood magic, the inky waters heaved and convulsed and finally split into twin canyons towering above the dumbstruck Israelites.

Just then Jim bolted to his feet and punched the air toward the east, blurting loudly, "They crossed over . . . *there!*" I watched his eyes plumb an imaginary line across the Straits into the eastern horizon, then stole a quick glance at Larry, who casually cocked an eye over his shoulder at the eastern skyline. Then, as if talking to himself, Jim said, "If *that's* where they passed through the sea, then Mount Sinai has to be . . . over *there*." He pointed to a distant ribbon of shadowy landfall, nearly invisible in the mottled, darkening sky: the west coast of Saudi Arabia. Until then, the legendary mountain where Moses received the Ten Commandments had remained in the background of our daily discourse.

"The children of Israel were trapped on *that* beach when Pharaoh approached," he continued. Larry and I turned to eye the narrow wedge of coastline in the flickering moonlight. It was hemmed in, just as Scripture says, "between the desert and the sea." Where we were anchored in the Straits, the narrowest span in the entire Gulf of Aqaba, one can easily see the Saudi coast. Jim turned around calmly and looked me square in the eye, grinning like a catfish.

"It's in Saudi Arabia, Bob," he declared, trying to be patient. "Bob, do you see it? Mount Sinai is in Saudi Arabia! Everybody thinks it's in Egypt, but it's not. It's in *Saudi Arabia!*" Excitement flared in his eyes. He stood by my side and put a firm hand on my shoulder. "Bob, I stood on the moon, but I can't get into Saudi Arabia. For us, the moon is Mount Sinai."

I stared out over the water, its burgundy waves lapping at the boat. Marine biologists say there is no body of water in the world so rich and diverse in underwater life as the Red Sea. An open Bible sat in my lap, its dog-eared pages rustling in the night breeze. I found myself thinking: *If the sea somehow dried up beneath us, we could walk across the straits to Saudi Arabia in a few hours.*

Then it hit me. A violent shiver shot down my spine. *What was I doing here?* What business did I have to be perched on a yacht near this historic breakwater, weighing the merits of a moment in time without equal, with a man who'd gazed at earth from space? My pulse raced. I turned westward toward the peninsula, the scene from the movie still unspooling in my mind. I saw the Israelites, paralyzed with fear, watching dust from Pharaoh's chariots rise in the south. I looked east into a Saudi horizon barely visible in the eventide haze. I could have sworn Jim and Larry heard my heartbeat throbbing against my rib cage. If Jim was right . . . if Mount Sinai *were* in Saudi Arabia, what did that mean for *me?*

A breath of a whisper passed calmly in the cool night. Call it serendipity, call it a premonition, call it a whisper from God. I knew in that instant why I had come to Egypt. I stood ill equipped, yet awash in an overpowering assurance that one day, *somehow*, I'd stand atop the real Mount Sinai.

Four

INTO THE KINGDOM

Six months after we returned to the United
States, our much-anticipated search for the
real Mount Sinai got firmly underway.
Preparations had taken some unnerving twists
and turns, but once things started rolling,
everything unfolded fast—though not the way
I had imagined. For one, Jim Irwin had
decided not to come along. He bowed out
early, a shocking development. I naturally
assumed that the three of us—Jim, Larry, and
I—would pool our wits and resources to find a
way into Saudi Arabia.

It didn't happen that way. Jim made some
inquiries, talked to some well-connected
politicians, congressmen, checked in with the
foreign consulates, and concluded he was far
too visible to attempt the trip. I resisted that
conclusion for a time, but sensed he was probably right. What chance, realistically, did a
high-profile astronaut stand of gaining legal
access to a country as hostile toward the West
as Saudi Arabia—for the exclusive purpose of

searching for the sacred mountain of ancient Israel? Saudi Arabia and Israel hate each other. What could be more detestable to Saudi Muslims than having an American astronaut discover Judaism's holiest mount in Mohammed's backyard?

In the end, Jim bowed out diplomatically. "Bob," he said, "Saudi Arabia is just too hard to get into. This search will require a very low-key operation, and I'd attract too much attention." Besides, he said, he was mounting another expedition to Mount Ararat and wanted me along. So I let it rest. All thoughts of Mount Sinai soon faded.

Then one afternoon a few months later, the phone rang at my office. Larry Williams pointedly bypassed the pleasantries. "Bob," he said curtly, "I'm thinking of going to Saudi Arabia to find Mount Sinai. Are you interested?"

What? *Was I interested?* Try shocked. Larry didn't even try to finesse the subject. He needed to know. *Now!* Did I want to join him on a foray into Saudi Arabia?

Words momentarily failed me. *Was I interested? Of course! But what's the catch?* After a brief pause, I asked bluntly: "How much is it going to cost?"

"I've got the money," Larry answered. "I'm paying for everything."

That's all I needed to know. I swallowed hard and said, "You bet. I'll go."

"Good, I'll be in touch," he replied, then hung up.

I could feel the adrenaline surging. *YES!* I felt honored that Larry would ask *me*, the lowly luggage handler on his star-crossed chariot search, on such a dangerous mission.

(Come to find out, he'd already asked a handful of others, but they turned him down flat. Saudi Arabia scared them off. One after another told Larry it was simply too dangerous. I just happened to be next on the list . . . and it was a pretty short list. Those who do this "adventure" thing know: if you're looking for a partner, there's no index in the Yellow Pages under "Explorer," no alphabetic resource guide for daredevils.)

Larry knew me, knew my role as vice president of Jim Irwin's High Flight Foundation, knew I was an ex-cop with some seasoning as an explorer. The way Larry saw it, we enjoyed one another's company—he could trust me in a tight squeeze and enjoy a few kicks along the way. The way I saw it, Larry and I intersected at a unique point in time. Now we faced an uncommon opportunity, the kind we'd both been preparing for most of our lives. When that moment arrives, you just know it. And you jump without thinking.

Larry clamped on target like a bull terrier. He was all business. Finding Mount Sinai had gripped his mind from that last night on the Straits of Tiran. Failing to unearth the chariot wheels had filled him with frustration, but already he was on the scent of something far bigger.

PREPARATION

I was beginning to have some doubts. When I asked Jim for his blessing, he offered his support, but also raised some sticky questions. Had I considered the gravity of what we were planning?

He likened it to the spirit of machismo needed to parachute from an airplane at ten thousand feet. "It's exciting," he confessed. "You picture yourself streaming majestically through the air like an eagle. But then you start learning about all the things that can go wrong: the chute might not open; wind gusts might tangle your cords; you might panic. A zillion things could happen to end your life." Jim knew I had a family and a good life in Colorado Springs. Before giving his blessing, he wanted to know: "Are you *really* prepared to enter a country where they cut people's heads off?"

Well . . . was I?

The next time I spoke with Larry, I asked some pointed questions myself. Like how, for starters, were we going to get into the country? We couldn't go as tourists; there *is* no tourism in Saudi Arabia. You either have a job beforehand—like thousands of foreigners imported for high-paying work in the service industry, or with one of the multinational oil companies—or you need someone important inside the country to officially invite you. Larry's response? "No problem." He had a friend in London, he said, Jack Trimonti, a fellow commodity trader who "knows a Saudi prince and is very well connected at the consulate. He says he can get us in." Larry seemed unconcerned.

As it happened, he'd already spent six months trying to obtain a visa, obtaining only consistent rejection. He tried to obtain our credentials conventionally at first, lobbying Saudi emissaries in Los Angeles, networking with Arab consulates, making endless phone calls, and explaining to anyone who would listen that, as a potential invester in Arab commodities, he needed to tour the Saudi countryside and meet the people. But no luck.

Our options finally narrowed to Jack Trimonti in London. Solely on the basis of Jack's assurances, Larry purchased airline tickets for us from L.A. to New York and on to Jedda, Saudi Arabia, where we'd fly to Tabuk in northwest Saudi Arabia. That's where our search would begin. Larry called one afternoon to say, "The countdown's on. Get your bags packed." But as the day of the flight neared, we still had no visas. Trimonti hadn't been able to secure us a sponsor; his Saudi prince flew out of town in his Lear Jet, winging to Scandinavia to see the Northern Lights. Now it was nail-biting time!

Our hopes lifted three days before our flight, when a fax, purporting to be from the prince, arrived at Larry's Los Angeles office. The note asked the Saudi government to grant Larry and I visas so we could do business in Riyadh. I took the fax, along with our visa forms and pictures, to L.A.'s Saudi consulate. They flatly rejected it, telling me in scolding, almost jeering tones that they could *never* accept a faxed copy of a letter. So we found ourselves back to square one with only two days to go. Our visa headache had turned into a code-red emergency.

We had tried, unsuccessfully, to get our visas the conventional way; now it was time to try something else. Enter a little ingenuity. Larry called Jack in London. "Catch a plane to London," Jack said. "I'll pick you up. It'll be quicker to work through the Saudi embassy here." So, at great expense, Larry forfeited our tickets to New York and hastily rerouted our itinerary through London. We left that afternoon. For the trip to succeed now, everything would have to run like clockwork. Larry had cleared his calendar months in advance and carved out days from his trading business to give us the minimum time we needed to conduct a reasonable search. If the trip didn't pan out now, it would be another year before we could try again.

We hopped a plane to London, where Jack met us and introduced us to his friend, Dimitrie, a tall, overweight, cigarette-smoking Greek. Dimitrie traded commodities like Jack and claimed to have Saudi friends in high places. A flamboyant, colorful character, Dimitrie calmly assured us we'd get our visas: "No problem! You'll be on your way to Jedda tomorrow."

I have always distrusted the phrase "no problem." So when tomorrow came and went and we still didn't have our visas, it hardly surprised me. Had Dimitrie perhaps embellished his friendship with his embassy contacts? Or maybe the contact didn't have the clout he claimed. Whichever was true, we didn't ask. We had put our fate in Dimitrie's hands, and that was that.

An embarrassed Dimitrie got angry. Determined to save face, in a clever stroke he rushed us to his office and programmed his fax machine to the prince's Saudi phone number, time, and country code. Then he faxed a note to a friend, and *voila*! The printout appeared to be a legitimate message from Saudi Arabia. Dimitrie then went to his file cabinet and pulled out a letter from the kingdom, conveniently printed on royal letterhead and bearing the prince's signature. Dimitrie told Larry to start typing another sponsorship letter as he worked the scissors and copy machine. He would get this thing to work, one way or another.

I could see what was happening and didn't much like it. "This isn't what I bargained for," I told Larry. The trip was taking a bad turn. In a matter of days we had gone from entering the country legally to concocting some wild fax scheme with a forged royal signature. I'd gone from thinking it was a sure bet to knowing we were taking our lives in our hands. Dimitrie seemed determined to drag us into some grossly illegal intrigue that could well get us killed. I watched skeptically as he made a copy of the letterhead and signature and affixed it to the new sponsorship letter. It looked, indeed, like the prince had written it himself. But when it came off the copier, the signature appeared blotchy and blurred. It didn't look real, and no one knew how to fix it.

I looked at Larry and said crossly, "I'm *very* uncomfortable with this. We could get in tremendous trouble." He stared back at me like I was a loon, then pulled me aside and asked point-blank: "Are you bailing out on me, *Bob?* I've spent a lot of money on this. If you can think of another way, say so now, but I need to know. *Are you in?*"

And that was it. At that moment I crossed over. I wanted it so bad! Thousands of miles from home, neck deep in an international intrigue, I felt as if my manhood were in question. I had wanted to keep everything legal and aboveboard, but it was too late. I bent to the pressure. "Yes, I'm in," I said with great anguish. Then I turned angrily to Dimitrie. "Give me the signature," I demanded. "If we're going to do this, let's do it so we don't get caught."

My investigator's mentality kicked in. I took the prince's inscription to the copier and enlarged it several times. Then, with a black pen, I carefully retraced it and colored in all the gaps and white spaces. Then I returned to the copier and reduced it to normal size. It looked perfect, bold and official, and set us to racing around, cutting, pasting, and correcting typos. We recopied the letter, transposed it over the king's signature and letterhead, then faxed it to the Saudi embassy with the preprogrammed Saudi time and country code. And incredibly . . . *it worked*! The embassy quickly faxed us back and told us to come down with our papers and passports—they'd have our visas ready by Monday afternoon. One problem: it was Thursday, and our flight to Jedda left on Friday. The offer didn't cut it.

Unwilling to waste four critical days, Larry began to pressure Dimitrie to use his contacts to get us airborne more quickly. "No problem, no problem," he said again in what had become the trip's mantra. He had *another* friend at the Saudi embassy who could clear the red tape. "Meet me at my office at ten in the morning," he said. "We'll go to the embassy, pick up your passports and visas, and you'll be on your way."

Eager to believe, we bid Dimitrie goodnight and returned to our hotel, hoping it was essentially a done deal. But at ten the next morning . . . no sign of Dimitrie. An hour passed. Finally Larry shrugged and said, "Forget about Dimitrie." We flagged a cab to take us to the Saudi embassy. We'd see what we could do on our own!

Our cabby, a guy named Peter, seemed a dead ringer for Steve McQueen (and just as cool). While keeping an eye on the angry, grid-locked traffic, he cocked his head to listen to our story. He seemed fascinated by it. When he pulled up to the

Saudi embassy, he said, quite unexpectedly, "Hurry up! Give me all your receipts and tickets stubs." Like nearly everyone else in London, Peter, too, had a friend at the Saudi embassy; and this one owed him a favor. Dazed and speechless, we stuffed our papers in his hands and followed him inside. Our flight to Jedda took off in two hours; time was slipping away.

Peter introduced us to his gambling buddy, an amiable Saudi whose eyes lit up when he saw our sponsorship communiqué from such a high official. With the bogus letter and Peter greasing the bureaucratic wheels, the Saudis treated us like royalty, serving us tea and handling us like VIPs. It seemed like a sweet dream that would soon burst—yet they gave us our passports *and* visas in an hour. And that was it. We had done it. *Why hadn't we gone to a cabby in the first place?* I asked myself.

Once outside, Larry and I hugged like long-lost sisters and let out a wild victory cheer that drew glares. But it was late . . . and rush hour. We turned to Peter and pleaded: "We've got forty-five minutes. You *have* to get us to the airport." And like Steve McQueen in *Bullitt*, he dodged and weaved through London traffic like a stunt driver, narrowly avoiding several collisions and dropping us at Heathrow Airport with twelve minutes to spare. Shaking our heads in disbelief, we awarded Peter the biggest tip I've ever seen and boarded the plane to Jedda. I wasn't pleased with how we'd accomplished it, but I had to admit, *something* was working in our favor. A rippling sense of elation rose in my heart. *This*, I said to myself, *is an adventure.*

Belted tight in my seat, however, my giddy mood soon clouded over. Over the intercom, staccato prayers in Arabic began. I looked around and realized the plane teemed with religious pilgrims bound for Mecca. We were the only Americans on board, citizens of one world invading the turf of another.

That's when the loneliness and uncertainty of fleeing everything safe and familiar for something utterly foreign and forbidding hit me. As Muslim prayers reverberated through the cabin, I began to pray too.

O Lord, don't let our little fiction get us hung in Jedda!

Five

THE LAND OF MIDIAN

The blood drained from Larry's face. He tried
hard to look calm, but his rapid breath, shiny
forehead, and pallid cheeks gave him away.
His stomach churned, same as mine. My heart
pounded so violently I thought it might pop a
valve.

We had deplaned at the international airport
in Jedda, Saudi Arabia, and now stood in line
at our first crucial check-through point. My
shoulders tightened like steel cables. A well-
trained young man of eighteen or nineteen
scrutinized each passport with a practiced disregard for time. He stared vigilantly into each
traveler's eyes, looking for the inappropriate
smile or nervous tick. I turned and looked at
Larry; I doubted his clammy pallor would fool
this young seer of souls.

Nagging questions seized me: had we covered
our bases? It was more sad than terrifying to
think that our quest for Mount Sinai might
end here. They might cart us off to prison or

stand us before a firing squad before we could claim our luggage.

I nudged Larry discreetly . . . gave him a wink. It was time to be cool. Larry winked back and, with a sheepish grin, took a deep breath. I summoned all my courage as he handed the armed inspector his papers; the young man keypunched Larry's information into the computer. Our moment of truth! A few seconds passed; Larry glanced at me with a raised eyebrow. The guard tapped more keys. Another minute of excruciating suspense, with no verdict.

Finally, the inspector raised his head and took a long, contemplative look at Larry, appraising him from head to toe. Feigning nonchalance, Larry stood there in a sort of exaggerated slouch and pretended not to notice. Then, without a word, the inspector handed Larry his passport and visa and pointed him toward the gate. He was *in!* I nearly let out a victorious "*Whooop!*"

Larry gestured to the guard that I was with him, and I, too, breezed through the gate. Our deception had worked; we were in the kingdom! We all but pranced to the terminal, scarcely looking at one another for fear we'd break out laughing. We felt triumphant, like two kids who had sneaked into the Super Bowl. Exhausted but far too excited to take a nap (although it was nearly midnight), we waited two hours for our plane to Tabuk, where the climactic phase of our journey would begin.

CRASH LANDING IN TABUK

What was up with our forty-five minute flight to Tabuk? We'd been in a holding pattern for more than two hours. Larry finally turned to me and said, "They're dumping fuel—it looks bad." His eyes told me we were, indeed, in trouble.

Why hadn't we landed? I could see Tabuk from my window—a smallish city with a population of no more than twenty thousand people. No other blinking lights lined up in the night indicating air traffic problems; no weather systems posed a problem. Larry took out his pocket compass, and we both watched as the needle slowly began to move. The plane was banking, ever so slightly. Over the next hour we made four huge circles in the desert, either to burn or dump fuel (a tactic used for rough landings). Was this our comeuppance? Had we made it through customs only to die in a plane crash?

I asked a flight attendant about the holdup. "Not to worry," she said. "No problem!" Now I *knew* we were in trouble. This same model jet had crashed in Sioux City. Was it the hydraulics system? Couldn't they get the landing gear down? Larry shifted nervously in his seat, repeating, "Bob, this is bad."

The plane finally began its descent, losing altitude at an alarming rate. With my stomach wedged in my throat, I could see the city lights getting closer and closer. The plane started to shudder and shake, then quake violently, throwing open bathroom doors. The wings thrashed and flapped like a wounded seagull. Any second, I feared, the entire fuselage would fracture. The runway lights appeared—I counted the flashing beacons of fifteen emergency vehicles positioned on both sides of the strip. Suddenly, when it seemed we were about three stories above ground, the pilot apparently cut his engines, and we dropped from the sky like a stone. We hit pavement with a crunching thud that knocked the wind out of me and jolted my neck and spine like a whipsaw. Mayhem erupted in the cabin: passengers were tossed about like fruit, screaming as their heads rammed into overhead bins. Luggage flew across the aisles like errant missiles. The plane careened down the runway to the wrenching sounds of metal grinding asphalt. The cabin quickly filled with the stench of burning rubber. Then, with a final, ear-splitting roar, the plane lurched to a stop at the far end of the runway.

Emergency vehicles, sirens squealing, instantly surrounded us. Firemen in silver asbestos suits swarmed about, aiming jets of foam and water at the plane's smoldering undercarriage. Through the plumes of smoke, I watched the emergency crews race into action. From my SWAT days, I could see they had an efficient, keenly coordinated operation. But then I caught a glimpse of something that made me cringe. I would've laughed—or maybe cried—if I hadn't been so terrified. Every single fireman, beneath his space suit and high-tech gear, was wearing *sandals*—lightweight leather sandals, like you'd see at a garden party. They'd cut out the bottoms of their rubber jackboots and raced out to fight a fire, Arab style!

Within moments an armed soldier burst into the cabin, shouting orders in Arabic. He herded us toward the exit, through a phalanx of guards who nudged and prodded us to keep moving to the bottom of the portable stairs. I turned to check out the damage to the plane's undercarriage when a guard slapped the small of my back with the flat of his rifle butt, then screamed as if he would shoot me on the spot. Apparently he didn't want me to see the craft's mangled front end and underbelly, with the wheel hub melted and twisted and bent grotesquely under the scorched chassis, the nose cone puckered and still smoldering from fire and friction. I marveled that we had survived.

Inside the terminal, a flight attendant told us the plane's wing flaps had malfunctioned, rendering the pilot unable to control either landing speed or altitude. Larry grimaced and whispered, "We're fortunate to have landed upright."

"I hope this isn't an omen," I replied, dead serious, as we collected our luggage. I was sick of surprises; already there had been enough close calls to last the entire trip. Nearly delirious from fatigue and nursing an acute case of jet lag, I hailed a cab, and we headed for our hotel: the Tabuk Sahara.

FINAL PREPARATIONS

The heat in Jedda—leaden and wet, like a damp wool sweater you can't take off—had nearly done us in. But at 2 A.M. in Tabuk, the temperature seemed surprisingly pleasant, not nearly as hot as I'd feared. It seemed almost balmy, not unlike the muggy California summers of my youth.

So this is Midian, land of Exodus, I thought. I had conjured up all kinds of images about this ancient terrain. Seeing it for the first time demystified those visions; I wondered how it had remained shrouded in mystery for so long. Larry and I believed this sweep of hill and sand was the true resting place of Mount Sinai. Had centuries of scholarship simply missed Midian's claims to the Exodus and the real Mount Sinai?

"Well, here we are," I said eagerly. It sent chills down my back to imagine that we were perhaps crossing ancient dunes once plied by the Israelites.

Relaxing in the back of a cab, Larry and I resumed a spirited dialogue we began back in the States. It seemed such a simple logic to us now, especially here. Our trip to Egypt had systematically dismantled the traditional view that Mount Sinai lay somewhere in the southern Sinai Peninsula (see Part Two). We knew that when the Israelites fled from Pharaoh and passed through the Red Sea, they declined to tarry in their enemy's backyard. Only one question remained: *Where did they go?* The Exodus trail we retraced pointed unequivocally to Saudi Arabia.

48

Approaching the outskirts of Tabuk, we revisited the facts, reminding ourselves that the Book of Exodus chronicled *two* distinct escapes from Egypt. The first occurred forty years prior to the famous Exodus, when Moses fled Goshen after murdering an Egyptian (Exod. 2:15). Four decades later, when Moses returned to Egypt to free the Israelites, he led them back to the land of his expatriation, to Mount Sinai . . . in Midian!

And where is Midian? Any biblical map shows Midian as present-day Saudi Arabia. Moses met his wife in Midian and lived there in quiet exile, tending the flocks of his father-in-law Jethro, a tribal chieftain prominently revered as the "priest of Midian" (Exod. 3:1). In Midian, Moses led a life of uninterrupted anonymity until the day something extraordinary happened: God spoke to Moses from a bush that glowed with fire but was not consumed. In Exodus 3:1–2 we read how Moses "led the flock to the far side of the desert and came to Horeb [or Sinai], the mountain of God. There the angel of the LORD appeared to Moses in flames of fire from within a bush." This is the first mention of Mount Sinai in the Bible.

The drive into Tabuk unnerved us. For some reason, thousands of towering, phosphorous lamps illuminated the highway. It was nearly 3 A.M., but one almost needed sunglasses. "I guess the Saudis aren't too concerned about the energy crisis," Larry quipped. I chuckled, for indeed, the sky blazed for miles around in an eery orange glow, seemingly for no other reason than to burn oil and drive up the price of Saudi crude.

Even more bizarre—as we entered Tabuk in the dead of night, the roads and highways bustled with frolicking humanity: teens tossing frisbees, kids riding bikes, skating, playing soccer, families enjoying picnics along the grass-lined medians and roadside parks. "What's going on?" I asked, dumbfounded. "It's 3 A.M." Our cab driver, an English-speaking Filipino, turned and explained, "It's the only time of day it's cool enough to be outside. The heat here is so intense during the day that people stay inside all day, sleeping. They come out to play only at night."

We checked into the Tabuk Sahara, threw our bags on the floor and collapsed; neither of us moved until the maid woke us up mid-morning with a loud knock at the door. Rested and refreshed, we ate a leisurely breakfast of unidentified Arabic meats, fruits, and juices and set up our command post next to the hotel's fifty-foot-long, turquoise-green swimming pool.

It was Saturday, a day of rest and preparation, a day to collect our thoughts and finalize plans for our desert sojourn the following day. We needed provisions, so we caught a cab into Tabuk, a drab, antiseptic town of gray-and-white modern cement buildings. Unfortunately, by the time we ventured out of the hotel, most stores had closed for noon-time prayers and wouldn't reopen until late afternoon. We scrambled to find a store that was just closing, and—practically elbowing past the flustered proprietor—proceeded to clear the shelves. We stock-piled enough crates of bottled water, canned meat, and fresh fruit to last several days. By day's end we had scrounged the town for everything we thought we might need: extra flash-lights, shovels, rope, gloves for climbing, brooms for dusting off artifacts. We even rented a little white Datsun pickup and bought enough jerry cans of gasoline to make it, in a pinch, back to Colorado. Our shopping chores completed, we retired to the pool to rehearse our strategy.

We spent the waning hours of daylight poring over maps, let-ters, and treatises. We reviewed Bible verses describing what Mount Sinai should look like and made a list of what should appear at the site (as well as what shouldn't). Then we quizzed one another ruthlessly.

We invented scenarios: What would happen if the truck ran out of gas? What if we got sick? What if one of us were cap-tured? We worked through every possibility and arrived at a guiding principle: No matter what happened, we'd stay together. *No matter what!* If we were arrested and one of us had a chance to escape, we'd stay together. If one of us were injured, we'd stay together, *then* find a way to safety.

By evening, we sensed we were ready. According to our maps, Jabal al Lawz lay roughly eighty miles northwest of Tabuk, into the desert. At last, the moment we had waited for had arrived. Tomorrow we would try to find the mountain!

Still, a piercing anxiety fell over me as we retired. As a police officer, I lived in a world where one radio call would bring help;

Larry thrived in a world where his credit card solved any problem. But here, in this world, we were winging it, utterly out of our element. It was like scuba diving in unknown waters, where the fish have the advantage. Neither of us knew a thing about desert survival; neither of us spoke or understood Arabic.

I tried to sleep, but my mind played and replayed a spinning montage of old Foreign Legion films, where the desert looms as a blistering-hot place of unquenchable thirst, merciless sandstorms, and murdering bandits. I dreamed we got stranded in a dune and had to crawl through the desert for help. There I was, lying next to a barrel cactus—nothing left but my bleached skeleton and a few tattered rags. Behind me, in the sand (like in the comic strips), lay a meandering trail of wobbly footprints; and my bony fingers clutched at an empty canteen.

Goodnight, Saudi Arabia.

51

Six

INTO THE DESERT

We checked out of the Tabuk Sahara at 6
A.M., high on testosterone, and drove north.
We knew Jabal al Lawz was one of the tallest
mountains in western Saudi Arabia, and a
topographical map showed us that, at 7,884
feet, it should be visible from some distance.
We followed the highway for two hours, arriving at our first landmark: the Al Kan gas
station. Our wilderness turnoff lay exactly four
miles north.

We drove four miles, but saw no exit, no
turnoff, nothing that could even loosely be
termed a road. We doubled back, retracing the
same tract of highway three times, but still
found nothing. On the fourth pass I told Larry,
"This is ridiculous. Let's get off." We agreed to
exit at the spot where we had seen a faint,
weathered impression of two tire tracks drift-
ing off toward the dunes. Within minutes we
found ourselves negotiating the floor of an
immense desert valley—a sandy plain that
split off into dozens of narrow forks and wad-

dies, each of which seemed to subdivide into dense clusters of winding ravines and stony ditches. Every fifty yards or so huge rocks, sand drifts, and sagebrush blocked our path.

We sought a series of odd-shaped rock outcroppings and other peculiar landmarks that were supposed to lead us to our only local contact, Ibraham Frich, a Bedouin sheep herder of some local prominence. Frich's tents were reported to lie near the base of Jabal al Lawz. If we could find Frich, we should be close enough to find the mountain without having to ask.

The terrain, jagged and jarring, was rumored to feature key landmarks: "a big rock that looks like an eagle," "a set of boulders that looks like an elephant," "a rock that looks like a turtle shell." Yet where were they? We passed scores of rock formations but nothing recognizable. "Are we on the right path?" we kept asking ourselves. One wrong turn—where one valley fingers off into dozens of little gulches—and you're hopelessly lost. With growing dread, we bounced and crunched through bruising ruts and scrub-filled ravines, bottoming out every few yards and fearing that at any moment we'd crack the oil pan and cook the engine.

Even worse, the hot desert breeze in our faces felt like pressing one's head into the mouth of a space heater. We rolled up the windows as tight as a coffin and tried to stay cool by pouring bottles of water over our heads. Soon we found ourselves coated with layers of muddy dust that clung to us like Velcro.

HOT SHEEP AND SLEEPY CAMELS

Wandering aimlessly, we soon discovered we weren't alone. We passed several small Bedouin encampments and observed in the distance clouds of dust from pickups hauling sheep, cases of supplies, and large tanks of water—the dreary motions of desert commerce.

We lumbered ever deeper into sheep country. At dozens of points we passed what looked to be huge beach umbrellas raised several feet off the ground and tethered by ropes to tall poles. Tightly bunched herds of bleating sheep huddled under each, trying gamely to stay cool under their little man-made islands of refreshment. It looked ridiculous—curious eyes and noses protruding from dense, stifling heaps of wool—yet signaled that this harsh land could indeed sustain flocks and herds, perhaps like those tended by the ancient Israelites.

This is also camel country. Stopping the truck at a parched wadi to relieve myself, I walked to a crescent-shaped mound of half-buried boulders. As I stood there daydreaming of rain clouds and mountain streams, I sensed the ground moving and falling away. I watched, immobile, as a tall, yawning camel rose from his hiding place and towered over me. Shaking off its mantle of sand, the beast, surprised by my presence, leaned in close to sniff my face and uttered a loud "BRRRAAAAPPPPPPP!" It somehow fit—nature's gesture of disdain.

Larry convulsed with laughter. "*That*," he said, heaving for breath, "was *unbelievable!*" With a weary shrug, I replied, "Partner, we've reached the point of no return. If we keep driving in circles, we're playing with fire." He agreed. By now we had taken so many blind turns that we had no clue where we were—or if we could find our way back. I felt a sense of mounting alarm. We decided to turn back and try to find *something*

55

recognizable as a trail marker. I pulled off the path to make a U-turn—and promptly got us stuck in the soft sand.

I wanted to curse the unseen forces of our misfortune. Our mission seemed about to blow up on us, but would a tantrum help? I gathered my wits, took a deep breath, and said, "Let's dig out!" Our options were simple: either get to work now or fulfill my nightmare of the evening before.

56

The truck had buried itself up to its axles in the sponge-cake sand, and our frantic efforts to free ourselves only got us stuck deeper. The slightest nudge on the gas pedal set wheels to whining, spraying jets of hot sand out the back like a geyser. The temperature read 120 degrees and rising. Our faces, plastered with the same grit that casts everything here in a dull, gray monochrome, took on the pallor of old cement. Shimmering waves of heat undulated over the sand like hot air over the coils of a broiler. Despite guzzling water by the gallon, our thirst still raged. We were lost, exhausted, and nearing desperation—and all before lunch.

SAND TECHNICIANS TO THE RESCUE

Hoping to create some traction, we dug deep trenches around the wheels and then stuffed branches, twigs and stones into the furrows. I tried to rock the truck back and forth, working the gas and clutch like a pipe organ, but we just sank deeper and deeper. Larry barked orders from the rear: "Put it in reverse!" "Give it some gas!" For an hour under the blazing sun, then two, we continued our desperate efforts.

Finally, in a frenzy to dig out, I let my fear of dying in the desert get the best of me. In a panicky, impulsive moment, I tried to *push* the truck out. Grabbing the rear bumper, I planted my feet and strained to lift the truck from the sand. Nothing budged. The second time I tried, my body arched and contorted, pushing, driving, refusing to quit . . . until something snapped. I'd slipped—or ruptured—a disc. It felt like ten thousand volts of electricity surged through my back; my lower spine felt afire, throbbing with white hot spasms, as if someone were using a red-hot poker to pry bone from cartilage. I couldn't move but sat propped rigid against a rock, fighting the urge to scream.

And the truck? Still stuck but now worse than before.

Now we were done . . . as simple as that. The desert had beaten us. Our whole plan depended on tenacity; dogged persistence was our trump card. We had faced dozens of instances when we could have (and likely *should* have) tossed in the towel. But Larry and I just kept pushing the envelope, shoving obstacles out of the way, bulldozing through problems. But *now* . . . our resolve had vanished, evaporated in the heat. Disoriented and probably in the latter stages of heat prostration, we sat dead in the sand while the desert devoured our truck. The sun bored searing holes through us, and our tongues seemed as dry as matchsticks.

Numb and disheartened, I looked at Larry as if to say, "*What now?*" He shrugged, crestfallen, and was about to say something when, from nowhere, a white Datsun pickup appeared from under the horizon. With no warning or sound, it rose like that sleepy camel and pulled in behind us, its back end full of gawking kids. We sat there, speechless. Was the heat making us hallucinate? We didn't know whether to laugh or cry, but suddenly we realized how ridiculous we looked.

On our Tabuk shopping spree, we had purchased the flowing robes worn by Arabs throughout the Middle East—jalabiyyas, they're called—as well as the familiar kufiyya headdress, with its 'agal (rope) headband. We had smeared our arms and faces with instant sun-tanning cream (the lotion that turns one's skin orange), and we'd taken great pains to convince ourselves we actually blended in.

Yet at that moment, standing next to our half-buried truck, wearing our filthy robes, faces the color of overripe pumpkins, we must've looked like space aliens. "What freakish zoo exhibit is *this?*" the children's faces seemed to ask. They tried to contain their amusement, but were soon pointing and laughing so hard I thought they'd fall off the truck. We were happy just to see some friendly faces. We proved to be affable clowns, laughing along, making funny faces, handing out oranges to everyone's delight. The driver (the children's dad, we guessed) wasted no time assessing our predicament. Ordering his sons out of the truck, they hastily removed the sticks and rocks from the trenches we dug and began rocking the truck back and forth, letting sand slip under the tires. One of the boys deftly stroked the gas pedal, and in less than five minutes the truck levitated from its sandy grave. It seemed a miracle; these Bedouin sand technicians had obviously gotten trucks unstuck for generations.

Almost forgetting about my injured back, I politely inquired where we might find Ibraham Frich. Using hand signals and exaggerated voice inflections, I managed to stammer: "*Ibraham Frich, does he live near here? Have you heard of him?*" The Bedouin smiled and indicated Frich tended flocks nearby. *Was it true?* Had our tortured course actually led us to our goal?

The man agreed to take us to Frich's camp. We piled in our truck and followed him over a large, flat ravine, then drove east for about twenty-five minutes. The path ended at a sleepy clearing where three tents, a half-dozen mangy dogs, some camels, and a pack of sheep under a big umbrella earmarked Frich's home. Our guide woke some napping shepherds, had a few words, and returned to inform us, with an apology, that Frich had left for the day. He wouldn't be back until late afternoon, but we were welcome to wait. Larry frowned, shaking his head. I took his cue and, against all sound judgment, asked the Bedouin to "please take us to *Jabal al Lawz*."

All smiles and laughter vanished. The Bedouin's countenance flushed dark, his gracious manner jettisoned. A look of fear crossed his face as he talked quietly with the shepherds, who indiscreetly jotted down our license plate number. Clearly, *something* about Jabal al Lawz was big-time off-limits to these folks.

We fought to reestablish rapport, offering more oranges to the kids, softening our manner, and striking up a jovial tone. As best we could, we tried to convince him we were mere tourists who wanted a closer look at some of the kingdom's taller mountains. After long and tense negotiations, we persuaded the Bedouin to take us to Jabal al Lawz. He motioned for us to follow him in our truck . . . *quickly.*

Leading us down a gentle slope and up and around a high, narrow ridge, we found ourselves parked, in less than five minutes, at the foot of a wide, sloping wall of granite. Our reluctant guide stepped from his truck and, crouching like an Indian scout, began crawling up the rock face. We followed him, staying low as he instructed, to a craggy crest overlooking a low, yawning plain. There, kneeling beneath the silhouette of a huge boulder, the Bedouin pointed toward something in the distance. We craned our necks to peer out over the lower valley, and . . . Yes! There it was—*the mountain*! Rising majestically into the sky, it displayed two sharp peaks and a large, graceful tree between the twin summits. We had arrived, finally, at Jabal al Lawz.

From a distance, its crown seemed awash in shadow. But how? The Midian sun nearly blinded us and not a cloud dotted the sky—what could this puzzling shadow be? Suddenly my heart started pounding. Was this towering peak, in fact . . . were we finally looking at . . . the *real* Mount Sinai?

SEVEΠ

JABAL AL LAWZ

The Bedouin, now visibly agitated, moved close to Larry and me and pointed toward the mountain. "*Jabal al Lawz,*" he whispered, like a spy sharing a secret password. Then, with a look of mortification, he slithered back down the rock slope and sat sullenly in his truck. Crouched behind the crest of the rocky knoll, Larry and I just stared. "That's *it*," Larry whispered. "Jabal al Lawz." There was something special . . . no, imperial about it. It wasn't its height; I'd climbed peaks that dwarfed it. I couldn't put my finger on it, but I detected a grandeur, a quality looming larger than life.

Suddenly Larry stood up, pointed toward the base of the mountain, and asked with alarm, "What's *that?*" I looked down and saw a fifteen-foot-tall, barbed-wire fence around the base of the mountain. It looked new, with galvanized poles planted at intervals in concrete footings.

Just then we heard the sound of an engine and turned to see the dust trail of the Bedouin's truck as it sped around a bend, out of sight. "I guess Bedouins don't believe in long good-byes," Larry grumbled. Our reluctant guide had abandoned us without a word. Just as well—yet the speed and abruptness of his departure left us with a nagging concern: might he be racing off to report us to local authorities?

Returning to our pickup, we coasted down into the massive, exposed basin to get a closer look. In a small clearing behind a hill, we parked the truck, got out, and walked to the fence. A large sign, white on blue, announced in both English and Arabic: "*No Trespassing Allowed.*" That it was notarized at the bottom by the Saudi "Minister of Antiquities" confirmed its status as a restricted archaeological site.

We stared at the fence for a long time. Had we really come halfway around the world only to be stopped by a *fence?* Peering inside the barbed wire, about a quarter-mile to our north, we saw a small concrete building. A small guardhouse, or perhaps a jail annex? The sight of it gave me chills. "This doesn't look good," Larry mumbled to himself. For the moment, it seemed, we were safe—no sign of Saudi police or armed Bedouin guards. Still, it didn't bode well for our mission. If this were really Mount Sinai, we had to somehow document a veritable treasure trove of hewn altars, pillars and ruins, and odd geologic formations. There was no way around it: we *had* to get inside the fence.

THE ALTAR OF THE CALF

When the people saw that Moses was so long in coming down from the mountain, they gathered around Aaron and said, "Come, make us gods who will go before us. As for this fellow Moses who brought us up out of Egypt, we don't know what has happened to him."

Aaron answered them, "Take off the gold earrings that your wives, your sons and your daughters are wearing, and bring them to me." So all the people took off their earrings and brought them to Aaron. He took what they handed him and made it into an idol cast in the shape of a calf, fashioning it with a tool. Then they said, "These are your gods, O Israel, who brought you up out of Egypt."

When Aaron saw this, he built an altar in front of the calf and announced, "Tomorrow there will be a festival to the LORD" (Exod. 32:1–5).

We spent the next hour poking about the fence's perimeter. A letter we carried (see chapter 23) alerted us to a series of pet-roglyphs—ancient rock etchings—located on a heap of rocks some distance from the mountain (a religious site with biblical associations?). But our directions—"from base of mountain, altar located east of second set of rutted tire tracks as they go up valley"—were no help. The rocks all looked the same, and so many tire tracks crisscrossed the area that we decided to split up to cover more ground.

Larry went north; I went south. But before I did so, I returned to the truck to grab my dog-eared leather Bible. It had become an unexpected source of comfort, a kind of moral support in this hostile climate. I wanted it with me. Besides, if we encoun-tered these ruins, I wanted to quickly compare them with Scripture. These petroglyphs—depicting various Egyptian-style

63

deities, bulls, calf gods—were said to resemble a Hebrew altar, a place of sacrifice.

I cringed at every step; at any moment waves of searing pain could rocket down my spine. I kept my eyes focused on the ground, paying close attention to each stride. One wrong move on a jagged stone or chuckhole sent stabbing spasms shooting up my neck and down through my fingertips. It was as if all of my old football injuries—the sprained elbows, dislocated shoulders, scarred knees, and herniated discs—were all back and concentrated into a quivering knot in the small of my spine.

I soon lost track of where I was or how far I had walked. Suddenly I began to notice something peculiar about the landscape. Gone was the gray monochrome of the surrounding desert. Quite the contrary: Jabal al Lawz sat in an alluring, pleasant valley covered with sagebrush and other tall grasses, where trees and wild flowers adorned gentle, sloping hillsides. Rock canyons suggested past or present streams and rivers. No doubt a million-plus Hebrew pilgrims could comfortably pitch their tents in this expansive tract, a high plateau of sage and chaparral. The more I observed, the more it struck me that the plain about Jabal al Lawz would make a great campsite, an impeccable, logical gathering place for Israel's assembled tribes.

I padded gingerly over another knobby rise and down to a shallow vale, finding myself navigating a welcome, cooling patch of protective shadow. Shifting my gaze upward, I saw . . . it. The hairs on my arms stiffened; goose flesh rippled up the back of my neck. It was an altar, a huge mound of stacked granite. I felt like a hunter who'd tracked fresh footprints through the jungle, only to find himself nose to nose with a bull elephant. I stood speechless in the shadow of an immense, mammoth-sized pile of boulders, stacked one on another in a loose yet calculated array.

Whatever this was, it wasn't there by natural consequence. It sat high in the otherwise pancake-flat plain, a solitary, custom-fit totem to bygone events. And it was encircled by a fence similar to that which girdled Jabal al Lawz. Here again, a sign posted in Arabic and English warned trespassers to stay out.

"Larry!" I cried out. "*Larry!* Over here!" In the time it took for my friend to appear, I inspected the size and configuration of the rocks. From every angle it remained an altar, unnaturally arranged, thick and imposing at the bottom, flat and smooth on top. To heft its large and unwieldy boulders into place would have required thousands of skilled, able-bodied workers.

Opening my Bible, I found Exodus 1:11, an account of the Hebrew slaves forced by their Egyptian masters into bitter, backbreaking labor in brick and mortar. In this workhorse capacity the Israelites "built Pithom and Rameses as store cities for Pharaoh." As I studied the altar, it struck me that Pharaoh's entire (former) workforce had assembled at the foot of Mount Sinai, workers skilled in the art of building cities and moving mountains. Certainly, enough of them had arrived in Midian to raise this modest (by comparison) dais on short notice.

Larry came huffing over the rise, his khaki shirt and pants shiny with sweat. "*Shhhh*," he said, scolding, as he approached. "Be *quiet!* I saw Bedouin guards and dogs over there behind the fence. The guards had *rifles*." He had also observed shepherds and flocks wandering the back side of the mountain. "We have to be careful," he repeated. "You can't just . . ." and his jaw dropped in mid-sentence. I waited silently as he stood there gawking at the altar, neck craned skyward, taking it in, until his face lit up in a boyish grin. "Oh my," he gasped. "*What have we here?*"

Silently we circled the heap of boulders, snapping photographs, noting its subtle features, stopping here and there to peer through the fencing. The contrast of the altar's shadows against the blinding sun made it hard, at first, to see them. But then, there they were, clear as day: ancient-looking petroglyphs branded into the smooth rock face. Larry saw it first, its horns forked like the handlebars of a Harley chopper; on another rock was a calf. But the most striking of all was the one we saw of a man holding over his head a calf, its spiraling horns like those of the ancient Egyptian Apis and Hathor bull gods. But *why*? Why *cattle*? Why *here*? This isn't cattle country. It is sheep country and had been for as long as men had walked these plains. Saudi Arabia has *never* been known for cattle—unless, of course, they were driven here by the fleeing Israelites.

I opened my Bible and read aloud from Exodus 32:2–5: "Aaron answered them, 'Take off the gold earrings that your wives, your sons and your daughters are wearing, and bring them to me.' So all the people took off their earrings and brought them to Aaron. He took what they handed him and made it into an idol cast in the shape of a calf, fashioning it with a tool. . . . he built an altar in front of the calf and announced, 'Tomorrow there will be a festival to the LORD.' "

Larry looked at me with a cagey smile and nodded. It was too early to make firm pronouncements, but the presence of these engraved paeans to Egyptian cow deities and men holding calves aloft, on such an obvious altarpiece, seemed a convincing bit of evidence. We couldn't help but wonder: *Had we really stumbled upon the altar of the golden calf?*

LONELINESS OF MIDIAN

By 6 P.M. the sun slowly began to sink low into a red, velveteen sky. It was one of the longest days of the year and just beginning to cool. With my throbbing back facing the east flank of Jabal al Lawz, I sat alone atop a tilting rock, riddled with pain and doubt, wondering if I'd ever get to climb the mountain.

Larry, on the other hand, brimmed with inspiration and energy. Once we inhaled a quick meal, my well-rested, newly refreshed partner wanted to climb the mountain *right then!* "We have enough time to reach the top before it gets dark," he said in a mildly taunting tone that reminded me of his sprint challenge. I declined. I *had* to. I had already taken a long walk, trying desperately to limber up my back, but it just cramped all the more. It humiliated me. My whole life I had dealt with pain: as a college running back, I learned how to pop my dislocated shoulder back into joint to keep playing; as a policeman, I had been banged up, beaten up, and kept working, kept pushing. But now, standing where Moses likely once walked, I had to wimp out. I apologized to Larry—but my back was not going to let me climb that mountain on this night. "If you want to go by yourself, go ahead," I said dejectedly.

Larry backed off. He saw how much pain I was in and didn't want to risk a one-man assault. His mood shifted. "Let's set up a campsite and regroup for the night," he suggested. "We'll rest and see how you feel in the morning." It was a wise move, back injury or not: we hadn't anticipated a whole set of variables, and we needed a night to plan our next move. It had been a long, punishing day and a wrong move now could prove fatal.

Our campsite sat in an S-shaped, sandstone ravine, a perfect spot with plenty of shade and cover, so no one could see us from the road. It gave us a clear view of the back side of the mountain, allowing us to familiarize ourselves with the terrain. So we camped for the night, planning to wait for morning. Then, if I were able, we'd dig under the fence, walk to the mountain, and make our ascent.

An unspoken suspense was building, and with it an energy and exuberance hard to suppress. Yet we had much work to do before we could pop the champagne corks. I knew from my days as a homicide investigator to keep my emotions in check. *Always let the evidence speak for itself,* I reminded myself. Tomorrow held the key to our success or failure.

I watched the sun—a massive, red ball of fire—melt into the Carolina-blue horizon. The desert had grown deathly still, without even the whisper of a breeze to break its stony silence. I glanced at my watch. It seemed I'd been sitting on that rock, motionless for hours, but the watch said—*what?*—only ten minutes had passed. Time stood still in Midian, dragging on drearily, monotonously. Five minutes seemed like five hours. Ten minutes seemed like an eternity. My back throbbed. I was cranky and bored out of my wits. I wished only for the day to be over.

I thumbed through my Bible, and it fell open to the passage describing how Moses tended Jethro's flocks for forty years prior to heading up the great Exodus. For four decades he led, fed, and protected flocks of dumb, bleating sheep. He was eighty years old when God finally called him "to the far side of the desert" and gave him his marching orders. *Forty years* in this vast, arid wilderness! In the distance I observed a shepherd tending a tiny flicker of a campfire and settling in his flock for the night.

That's when I realized: God used this harsh land to prepare Moses. He didn't use a big university or a military academy; he used a tiresome desert and a bunch of brainless sheep. Boredom prepared Moses for that stubborn flock of Hebrews.

And there I sat—ten minutes on a rock and ready to scream. Yet all day long I had felt an unusual stirring, an unsettling sense that, just maybe, God was using an infernal desert and unyielding pain to forge something new in me. In deep silence I chafed against a heaviness that cut to my soul. I wasn't ready for this moment. Unlike Moses, I wasn't equipped to stand on sacred soil. Sitting on that rock, I understood, sadly, that I wasn't desert forged for this once-in-a-lifetime opportunity.

What would the coming hours bring? I had no idea. Would I be ready to climb that mountain as dawn clambered its way over the desolate frontier? Or was my journey over? Nearly two years of intense preparation, effort, and intrigue had boiled down to these few terrible hours of uncertainty. And yet—I hoped that I, too, might still find my destiny on this far side of the desert.

Eight

ON TOP OF THE WORLD

Dawn breaks quickly in the desert. Just before the sun's rays stretch across the desert floor, the heat slaps you like an open hand. Forget about any soft transition from the predawn chill. Instead, think instant, prickly discomfort and another relentless day of withering heat. On our first morning at the foot of Jabal al Lawz, the sun peered abruptly from behind an ink-black horizon, awaking us promptly at a quarter to six.

Larry slept on the ground beside the truck, his high-tech, Mylar space blanket crinkling and crackling at the slightest wisp of a breeze—yet another annoyance that kept me tossing and turning most of the night. Fear of snakes had prompted me to sleep in the pickup. I stretched my legs out one door and rested my feet on three boxes of water stacked outside—the worst night's sleep ever. But the prospect of lying at snake level in poisonous-asp country was beyond consideration.

I stood and tested my back. It felt better, though not healed. It still throbbed and ached, but the sharp pain was gone—a minor miracle considering my fitful night's sleep. It seemed fate had decided I would climb Jabal al Lawz.

After a quick breakfast of dehydrated fruit and bread, we filled our packs with water bottles, cameras, film, and protein bars, and shuffled across a thin stretch of exposed valley to the base of the mountain. Unlike the front (or east) side of the peak, the mountain's back side lies open and accessible. We planned to climb the back and come down the barricaded front (where most of our archeological interest lay), knowing we must make it both ways before the sun rose too high. We wore khaki clothing as a camouflage against the sandy terrain. We knew to keep a low profile—but sooner or later, we figured, we'd be seen by Bedouin patrols stationed nearby. Thus morning was our ally.

We arbitrarily chose a path up the hillside from among the spiderweb of trails fanning out from the base, then set a brisk pace up a surprisingly tame gradient. Jabal al Lawz isn't a big mountain, and Larry and I had both done a fair amount of technical climbing, so despite an occasional back spasm, the hike proceeded without incident. Sharp, jagged rocks and stinging briers made us glad we had worn heavy leather gloves. I pictured Moses, eighty years old when he ascended the peak for the first time, marching to the top without much difficulty.

Only once did we backtrack due to steep, impassable cliffs. But then we quickly returned to our course, scrambling up an alluvial fan of loose gravel that ascended into a twisting, upward-sloping ravine and through fields of huge boulders and unstable scree. We marched with a sense of urgency, as if every step were sacred and every pebble a miracle of creation. When the trail dissolved near the top, we clambered up the final pitch as best we could—one foot in front of the other, sometimes hand over hand—skirting flimsy rows of narrow ledges and stretching our bodies past sharp spires and fat outcroppings. Once we tiptoed along a slick granite wall angling out over a sheer forty-foot drop-off. Yet our growing excitement banished any sense of caution.

By 9 A.M., two hours into our climb, we approached the true summit: twin, snub-nosed peaks separated in the middle by a broad, rock-strewn bowl pitching down like an open-air amphitheater. With each footstep we wondered if we were setting foot upon the stage where the most extraordinary drama in human history unfolded. As we strained over the last, flinty hogback, we glimpsed a spectacular vista stretching out from the desert below. As the tallest peak in the area, Jabal al Lawz offers the privilege of gazing down upon the whole region. Our eyes drank in a polychrome lacquer of purple, yellow, and orange hills, flaxen valleys, and taupe plains fixed in an ageless panorama of wind-and-sand-sculpted shapes and textures. On this clear morning, we could see hundreds of miles in all directions: to the west lay the faint, slate-tinted coast of the Red Sea; to the north and south, majestic, rugged mountain ranges bounded by perpetual desert.

FURNACE OF FIRE

Cresting a final stair step of crumbling sandstone terraces, Larry asked, "Do you think maybe we're the first people—certainly the first *westerners*—to reach this summit since the time of Moses?" I smiled. It was a fair bet. The peak had tantalized our imaginations across oceans and continents, and now, it seemed, we'd arrived.

We had agreed to touch the summit at the same time, a silly "all for one and one for all," mountain-climber thing. But we were a *team*, and it seemed important to reach the top together. At the last step we hesitated, looked at each other and laughed, then counted in unison—"*One, two, three!*"—before stomping our right boots on the summit with a swashbuckling flourish.

It was celebration time, a moment to revel in the fact that, in all probability, we were standing on one of the holiest places on earth. We took several minutes to slap backs and congratulate each other, snap pictures, and drink it all in. At eight thousand feet the air had a fragrance and texture all its own. It smelled . . . how to describe it?—*transcendent*. Were we not standing where Moses received the Ten Commandments? Was this not a place unique to any other, where God commiserated with man in a season of unprecedented intimacy and fearsome wrath?

Larry whipped out a piece of paper and wrote a note to future travelers, extending our greetings and giving the time and date of our arrival; then he placed the note in a small glass bottle and buried it under some rocks. I thought it an excessive gesture, but for Larry it sealed the deal—a time capsule for posterity.

I had my own business. I pulled from my pack a little tube containing a rolled-up American flag, one I'd taken with me around the world (I got the idea from Jim Irwin, who brought flags back from the moon). I had Larry snap a picture of me with the flag on the summit, hoping, one day, to pass it on to

my kids. I opened my Bible and wrote an inscription commem-
orating the day with a Scripture verse, Exodus 19:20: "The
LORD descended to the top of Mount Sinai and called Moses to
the top of the mountain."

And then I remembered. In all the bustle I had failed to look
for the one feature that had gripped us from a distance: the
strange, dark crown that shrouded the summit like a permanent
shadow. Glancing about I saw that the entire surface where we
stood appeared stained, or tinted, a deep, unnatural black. The
rocks, even the dirt, had a shiny black pigment, like polished
obsidian—a startling effect. Seeing it from a distance was one
thing, but this genuinely baffled us. We stood on what
appeared to be a vast vein of exposed coal, all within a few
paces of the top. *What could cause such a thing?*

The sun continued to rise. No doubt Bedouins below were
dressing and steeping their breakfast tea. Morning was slipping
away, so we scurried about collecting as many loose rocks (for
future laboratory analysis) as our packs would hold. I noticed
Larry seemed utterly mystified, and at one point quipped: "This
has *got* to be a volcanic peak." There was only one way to find
out.

"If it's volcanic," I said, "then the rock inside will be black,
too." I picked up a piece of charred rock the size of a water-
melon, lifted it high over my head, and slammed it on the sharp
edge of a boulder. It cracked clean, and we leaned in close to
look: an exterior of melted stone, slick black like cultured glass,
encasing a reddish-tan core. The interior rock was ordinary
brown granite! "Well," Larry said after a long pause, "I guess
that answers *that* question."

Goose bumps bristled on the back of my neck. What type of heat could melt surface rock to a black marble glaze—smooth to the touch like buffed opal—yet leave the underlying granite intact? Clearly, something unnatural, intensely hot, had torched the mountaintop. But what kind of heat is potent enough to charbroil solid rock, leaving the marrow medium rare? Handling the rocks like fine china, Larry kept asking, "What could *do* that?" An iron smelter? An atomic forge? A laser cannon beamed from a satellite?

As I beheld the melted rock, a passage leapt to mind of a mountain "covered in smoke." I flipped open my Bible to Exodus. "Here it is," I said. From Exodus 19:16–19, I read aloud the account of how, three days after the Exodus party arrived at Mount Sinai, the mountain was mysteriously cloaked in a "thick cloud," the skies above filled with thunder and lighting. I read how a "very loud trumpet blast" nearly scared the Israelites to death, causing "everyone in the camp [to] tremble." Moses then led the people out of the camp to assemble at the foot of the mountain. And as I read the following text, Larry's mouth fell open: "Mount Sinai was covered with smoke, because the LORD descended on it in fire. The smoke billowed up from it *like smoke from a furnace*, the whole mountain trembled violently" (Exod. 19:18–19, emphasis added).

I kept reading. Once again, in Exodus 24:17, the glory of the Lord appeared to the Israelites "like *a consuming fire* on top of the mountain" (emphasis added). I tried to wrap my mind around this haunting word picture. The implications seemed clear: there *should* be concrete evidence of some fiery activity on top of the real Mount Sinai. *And here it was*, plain as day—the permanent inscription of God's devouring presence. The blackened rock had become a holy handprint for the ages. God placed his signature in heavenly flames in a fashion so electrifying, so stupefying, that man's proud logic and science would be hard-pressed to explain it.

God, it seemed, had tucked his mountain away in a closed society where all things sacred are protected against the kind of cheap exploitation we saw in Egypt. Small wonder tourists flock to the peak at St. Catherine's—it was a decoy! The real Mount Sinai had been completely veiled to civilization's prying eyes.

Seeing this rock, holding it—yes, even *smelling* it—sent chills of wonder down my back. But my wonder quickly turned to dread. At once, I knew why the Israelites became so frightened that they begged Moses to speak with God while they retreated to a safer distance. I understood for the first time that an unruly people cannot bear the judgment of a holy, omnipotent God. Then what of me—the unruliest intruder of all, standing there robed in guilt? The sudden shame nearly buckled my knees. I felt as if I were free-falling in an elevator shaft. "Do you feel anything strange?" I asked Larry. "Yeah," he replied, his face pale despite the sunburn. "This is weird . . . *really* weird."

My elation vanished, swallowed up by bitter regret. *Oh, my God*, I thought. It all flooded back: the forgery and deceit, the self-seeking stubbornness, the trampling of all restraint to enter the kingdom and bully our way to this sacred soil. *What are we doing here?*

I hadn't earned this privilege. I was trespassing. I recalled the stern admonition: "Whoever touches the mountain shall surely be put to death" (Exod. 19:12). The night before I had glibly dismissed the text—but now my heart was pounding. I felt sick. I believed at any moment a bolt from heaven would strike me down. Without thinking, I turned to Larry and barked an order: "Let's go—*NOW!* We have to get off this mountain!"

Nine

TERROR AND HOPE

I stood stiff as a statue, scared to move even a toe. Convinced I was standing where Moses once walked, my wonder turned to shame, then paralyzing fear. I felt naked—the audacity of slugging down Gatorade and munching M&Ms where Moses once "was there with the LORD forty days and forty nights without eating bread or drinking water" (Exod. 34:28)! *He* was preparing to receive the Ten Commandments, while *I* . . . I was nothing but a cocky ex-cop in hiking boots, sating a thirst for adventure. I wanted in that instant to be a million miles from Jabal al Lawz. But since we had a substantial hike ahead of us, I tried to calm myself.

Sure that the hand that melted granite could snuff me out like a match, I prodded Larry: "C'mon, let's go! We shouldn't be here." Larry placed the lens cap back on his Nikon. "I guess I have all the pictures we need of the top," he said hesitantly. He turned to see my gray pallor. "Are you all right?" he asked.

"Yeah," I said, averting my gaze. "I'll be fine." I was unable, or unwilling, to convey the terror gripping me.

We began a cautious descent down the mountain's exposed front side, keeping one eye fixed on the plain below for signs of human activity. My eyes darted about, fearing an ambush from warlike Bedouins crouched behind the next crag. Larry, on the other hand, seemed the picture of composure, quite pleased and unruffled by our mountaintop exploits. "Wasn't that incredible?" he kept repeating. But I felt weak, light-headed, barely able to balance myself on the loose slope. As a cop I had faced death countless times, but this was different. This was a breath-stopping, hair-whitening, wholly unfamiliar fear of God.

Shuffling on hands and feet across the slippery mountainside, we searched for a trail down, pausing briefly at the bowl-shaped amphitheater below the pinnacle. What exactly *was* this rock-hewn basin in the sky? A hidden plateau, easily two football fields long, sheltered massive boulders, each larger than a big house. Just below the second peak sat a peculiar, triangle-shaped monolith formed by two huge rocks tilted oddly against each other, fused together at the top in the shape of a V. In the crook—or cleft—of the V stood a lone almond tree, planted firm like a flagpole. I couldn't help noticing that this cleft looked just wide and deep enough for a man to lie down inside. I glanced at Larry, his expression blank.

I opened my Bible and turned quickly to Exodus 33. I read how Moses, conferring with God in the Tent of Meeting, asked boldly to see the glory of the Lord. God graciously consented, saying, "I will cause all my goodness to pass in front of you, and

I will proclaim my name, the LORD, in your presence. . . . But . . . you cannot see my face, for no one may see me and live" (vv. 19–20).

And then God added, "There is a place near me where you may stand on a rock. When my glory passes by, I will put you in a *cleft* in the rock and cover you with my hand until I have passed by. Then I will remove my hand and you will see my back; but my face must not be seen" (Exod. 33:21–23, emphasis added).

81

I looked up; not forty feet away sat a pronounced cleft in the rock. Was it just *a* cleft? My mind began to spin, fancying this hole to be the cleft where God revealed his glory to Moses. As I did so, my strength returned, the weakness left my knees, and I felt suddenly uplifted, revived. Seeing this small fissure bolstered me, reminded me of a God who wasn't only a deity to be *feared*. In a flash, the cleft symbolized for me an unparalleled moment of intimacy; Moses had been shown God's favor and was rewarded with a rich, supernatural friendship like no other. As Larry poked about the rocks, I mused what it would be to speak with God face-to-face or see his glory descend "in a cloud" over me, like a blanket. For Moses it must've been joyous, euphoric, for it left him with a countenance so radiant that it frightened the Hebrews. Thereafter Moses wore a veil in public (Exod. 34:29–35). "I'll bet that's it!" I told Larry—"the cleft in the rock." Larry nodded. As we headed down the mountain, I heard him mutter a barely audible "*Wow*."

THE SPLIT ROCK AT HOREB

Halfway down the rocky face we found a spacious, table-flat ledge concealed behind a tuft of bushes—the protected vantage we needed to survey the front slope. We laid out our cameras, telephoto lenses, and binoculars, and set to work, running down a checklist of man-made and natural features that should be present if Jabal al Lawz were the real Mount Sinai. First, we looked for traces of a river. Deuteronomy 9:21 speaks of a brook or river on Mount Sinai, where Moses disposed of the crushed remains of the golden calf. He ground the idol to powder and threw it into a "stream that flowed down the mountain."

Looking north, not twenty feet from our hidden perch, we saw it: a large ravine snaking down the mountain. An ancient riverbed? The meandering channel emanated from the mountain's west face, where it curled back around and pitched steeply down the east-facing slope, emptying discreetly into the plain. The ancient watershed—a chalky, blister-dry remnant of a bygone wellspring—was filled with large, water-polished boulders, clear evidence of a fast-rushing torrent. In a land that receives half an inch of rain per decade, it was proof that a stream of some magnitude had once caressed these rocks.

The channel's width and depth suggested it had played host to a cascade large enough to serve an army—a trait of no small importance. For when Moses struck the rock, the resulting flow didn't merely trickle or drip; Scripture speaks of an enormous volume of water surging from the rock at Horeb:

> "He brought streams out of a rocky crag
> and made water flow down like rivers" (Ps. 78:16).

And again:

> "When he struck the rock, water gushed out,
> and streams flowed abundantly" (v. 20).

"Water gushed out; like a river it flowed in the desert"
(Ps. 105:41).

These verses make clear that when Moses struck the rock the water erupted like a great geyser, creating a wide riverbed like the one we observed zigzagging down the face of Jabal al Lawz.

We checked the riverbed off our list.

But then . . . something we hadn't expected (and didn't recognize at first) peeked at us from behind the ridge. It sat in a shallow depression at the mouth of the ravine—a towering pillar of rock, split laser-fine down the middle, nineteen inches wide from top to bottom. Its appearance alone staggers the imagination, but the rock's implausible berth at the crown of the ancient headwater raises gooseflesh. It appears as if the riverbed sprang from the rock itself, as from a spigot.

"He split the rocks in the desert and gave them water as abundant as the seas" (Ps. 78:15, emphasis added).

Was it . . .? Could *this* be the rock that Moses struck?

The Bible says that after crossing the Red Sea the Israelites spent several days in the desert, where they became weary from thirst. Quarreling with Moses, they demanded, "Give us water to drink." In a fit of despair, Moses pled with God, "What am I to do with these people? They are almost ready to stone me." God answered: "Take in your hand the staff with which you struck the Nile, and go. I will stand there before you by the rock at Horeb. Strike the rock, and water will come out of it for the people to drink" (Exod. 17:2–6).

And here before us stood a massive column of granite split down the middle like a loaf of bread.

But there's more. Rubble at the foot of the rock had been scorched ebony black, just like the summit—the only other spot on the peak where the phenomenon occurs. Could it be the melted residue of God's presence? For when God said, "I will *stand* there before you at the rock at Horeb," it can be assumed that his glory was manifest in much the same way it was on the summit—in unquenchable, devouring fire. "Fire goes before him. . . . The mountains melt like wax before the LORD" (Ps. 97:3, 5). If God indeed stood with Moses at the rock of Horeb, shouldn't we expect exactly such a blackened patch at the base of the rock?

(We were able to confirm the find only after reviewing a startling set of photographs taken of the site by an American couple, Jim and Penny Caldwell, who lived and worked in Saudi Arabia.)

The split rock and its blackened base remain one of the startling features on a mountain that seems nothing less than a shrine to Mosaic Law and testament. Unfolding before us, like a proud, preening peacock, stood a sand and granite memorial to the great Exodus.

THE CAVE OF ELIJAH

From our sheltered perch we turned to scan the upper peak once more. Had we missed anything? The sun, now high in the sky, bathed the peak in a brilliant glare. Larry studied the upper heights with his binoculars while I reloaded the camera. After several moments he shouted, "There! Just below the second peak." I turned, squinting into the sun, and saw a cave, sheltered beneath the lip of the plateau. It lay not fifty yards from where we stood.

Could this be the cave of Elijah? First Kings 19:8–9 speaks of a cave on Mount Sinai used by Elijah to hide from Jezebel: "He [Elijah] traveled forty days and forty nights until he reached Horeb, the mountain of God. There he went into a cave and spent the night." We could have kicked ourselves for not seeing this crucial landmark earlier, when we were coming down from the summit. Who knows what petroglyphs it might contain? Only the fear that we might already have been spotted from below kept us from climbing up to investigate. It would have to wait for another trip.

STONE MARKERS

Time grew short. We riveted our attention toward the front slope and spent the next hour scrutinizing the mountainside. We might never have another opportunity like this; we didn't want to blow it. Gradually a scintillating array of features, parceled strategically about the mountain, began to emerge. Training our gaze first to the surrounding plain, we saw what looked to be a series of orderly piles of sun-bleached rocks encircling the front side of the peak. We recalled bumping into a couple of these the day before but misidentified them as Bedouin burial mounds. Now, from our elevated position, we could see they were stone *markers* of some sort, arranged in four-hundred-yard intervals in a perfect semicircle about the mountain.

My pulse raced as I rifled through Exodus, stumbling on verse 19:12, where the Lord ordered Moses to "put limits for the people around the mountain and tell them, 'Be careful that you do not go up the mountain or touch the foot of it. Whoever touches the mountain shall surely be put to death.' " Were these orderly-arranged stands of rock in the plain those sacred markers? Were we observing the work of Moses' own hands?

We lost ourselves in the heat of the moment, giddy as kids running amok at Disneyland. Each of us pointed and yelped, "Look over *here* . . . Look over *there* . . . What does *that* look like to you?" It all seemed beyond comprehension. Mount Sinai was revealing itself to us.

TWELVE PILLARS OF ISRAEL

"*Oh my God!*" Larry whispered in my left ear. "Check *this* out!"

"What?" I shot back, jerking my head to see what other prize had appeared. Larry calmly pointed at the base of the mountain. "Look down there," he said, eyes glued to his binoculars. "You're not going to believe it."

Sitting near the mouth of the ravine, nudged gently against the bluff, stood an angular stone altar—V-shaped and clearly manmade. Its tip nuzzled into the fold of the ridge, and its wingspan, slanting out at forty-five degrees, measured perhaps 120 feet. No doubt about it, it was an altar of some sort, badly weathered and crumbling in spots, with a height of five feet and a depth of about twenty feet. The remains of its center support wall ran the length of both wings of the V. Right beside the altar, almost in a straight line, appeared to be the hewn stumps of stone pillars, toppled over and broken in sections. Most lay near the altar.

I flipped pages furiously, wracking my memory, searching for relevant passages. Then I found it: Exodus 24:4–5, a remarkable description of what appeared to be standing before us: "Moses . . . got up early the next morning and built an altar at the foot of the mountain and set up twelve stone pillars representing the twelve tribes of Israel. Then he sent young Israelite men, and they offered burnt offerings and sacrificed young bulls as fellowship offerings to the LORD."

This must be it! An altar, sitting precisely at the foot of the mountain, built for worship. Breathlessly I counted the pillar stumps: *twelve*. "Oh my Lord," I blurted out, "this is the altar and pillars where the men offered burnt sacrifices to God!" Larry snapped away with his telephoto lens, muttering under his breath, "This is incredible. This is amazing!"

And so it was. So much so that I did a quick mental inventory to make sure it was real. *Blackened, scorched peak . . . ancient riverbed . . . split rock . . . massive stone altars . . . pillars . . . sacred markers . . . a curious cleft in the rock.* It was all there. What more evidence did we need? They could have filmed *The Ten Commandments* here without moving a stone.

If we had spotted but one or two of these unique features, I might have entertained some doubts. Each feature—the scorched mountaintop, the man-made altars, the petroglyphs, the pillars, the stone markers—was stunning, even electrifying, in itself. But their *sum* witnessed to the site's authenticity. There was nothing subtle about Jabal al Lawz. The mountain burst with the kind of empirical evidence I coveted in a criminal trial.

As I stared into the plain, I imagined the flickering glow of thousands of Israelite campfires warming the valley; I saw Hebrew children playing beside the tents, flocks, and livestock kneeling beside a huge reservoir carved into the plain. It was like being transported back in time to stand face-to-face with players in the most amazing story ever told. It was almost too much to bear. Here on Jabal al Lawz, set out like greeting cards on a shelf, sat a three-dimensional Bible encyclopedia of classic Judaism.

While Larry clicked away, whispering to himself, "This is *unbelievable*," something else stirred inside my own heart. My skin began to crawl once more at the thought of intruding where God breathed forth Israel's ancient system of law. How could we dare to *be* here?

This time, however, the sensation didn't stop there. From this gloom blossomed a lightness of heart, a brightness of spirit, shimmering with . . . *hope*. I had witnessed Truth! Raw, unedited Truth. And when it presented itself, faith entered my heart, just as sure as those rocks were burned black. It was suddenly *there*, first in a trickle, then like a dam had burst. It came from deep down, as from a spring. Yes—like a spring of living water. Every Sunday sermon I'd ever heard pulsed to life. The unbelievable stories: *Moses . . . the Exodus . . . the Red Sea . . . Mount Sinai . . . the Ten Commandments . . . Abraham . . . Elijah . . . Jesus!*

That's when I knew, in a moment simple and quiet: *It's all true.*

Ten

SECRETS OF AL-BAD

We scurried down Mount Sinai's east face (no longer Jabal al Lawz to us), exhausted but exhilarated. The exploration had succeeded gloriously. The features we'd observed, the photographs we'd taken, would make a convincing case that we had found the *real* Mountain of God.

Well past noon we swept the valley floor once more with our binoculars, making sure no other unusual features lurked below. Then we bounded off the mountain, barreling straight down at points and sliding a good bit of the way on our seats. We skidded to a stop at the bottom with gaping holes in our pants. From there we sprinted past the last jagged ramparts to exit at the peak's open back side.

We walked briskly through a washboard basin of dry washes and stubble-filled wadis to our campsite a mile away, ever mindful of Bedouin patrols. We took great pains to keep our heads low, below the bush line. On the way we found ourselves passing scattered groves of odd, thorny trees. On closer inspection, we realized they were acacia trees, the kind cited in Exodus, whose wood was used to build the sacred Tent of Meeting and its contents. Camped at Mount Sinai, Hebrew craftsmen, at God's detailed instruction, built the ark of the covenant, the table it sat on, the altars of incense and burnt offerings—even the sacred tent poles and crossbars— from acacia wood. I was surprised we hadn't noticed them before. We took several pictures to document our find . . . yet another in a succession of converging puzzle pieces.

Three-quarters of a mile into the plain, we thought we were home free. For the first time in days I allowed myself to relax and enjoy a sunny walk through a unique countryside. Suddenly, from our left—*voices*. Then a loud gunshot echoing through the wadi. "Oh man, what now?" Larry said, scanning the thicket. We walked a few more feet, stopped and waited. From the dense brush came a loud shout in Arabic, as if someone were yelling "*STOP!*" We stepped from the gully into a small clearing, where two Bedouins in military-issue garb immediately confronted us. The older, taller one cradled a large, single-shot, twelve-gauge shotgun. "Let's just try to stay cool," I whispered with a huge lump in my throat. Before us stood the walking embodiment of our worst fears: armed Saudis in uniform.

Smiling warmly and bidding them a cheerful "marahaba" (Arabic for hello), we waited to see what would happen next. We weren't sure if they were soldiers on patrol or simply bandits looking to steal our expensive equipment and cut our throats. Their baffled glances told us they didn't know what to make of us: two filthy, sweaty, sunburned Americans strolling about their desert.

Larry and I used the confusion to our advantage, employing humor and smiles to keep things light, trying to appear as friendly as possible. We laughed long and loud and took their pictures, showering them with offers of food and water. They refused our candy bars, but the tall one—an unshaven, ragged-looking character with terrible teeth—happily drank the last fuzzy dregs from our water bottles. Staying close to the guy with the rifle (it's more difficult to shoot someone at close range), we tried to loosen them up with silly antics. Finally, Larry cut to the chase—he gestured toward their gun and mimicked a man shooting birds from the sky, shouting "Bang! Bang! Bang!" They laughed and nodded as if to say, "Yes, we are hunters!"

My heart slowed a beat. Maybe they were neither soldiers nor bandits but simply two young Bedouins shaking the brush for quail. (In an interesting echo to Exodus 16:13, we scared up several large coveys of these short-tailed birds—descendants, perhaps, of the quail God rained down on the Israelite camp near Mount Sinai?) Carefully gauging their response, we smiled and waved, as if to say good-bye, then started walking toward the campsite. Our fears subsided when they strolled off in the opposite direction, disappearing behind a stand of acacias. Larry and I made a dash for the truck, anxious to avoid any more impromptu meetings with armed Bedouins.

Our relief didn't last. As we crested the final knoll overlooking our campsite, our hearts sank when we saw another pickup parked beside ours. "Looks like trouble," I told Larry. We climbed down to the edge of our camp to find our two Bedouin friends rifling through our boxes and suitcases and throwing all our papers and notebooks from the glove box. It looked like a scene from Disney's *Tarzan* movie—mad apes flailing their arms and throwing clothes, raising a clamor and making a mess. With a shudder I concluded they *were* soldiers after all, sent to search our stuff and arrest us for trespassing. Either that or they meant to rob us and shoot us and leave our corpses to rot—lousy options both.

92

Luckily, we'd buried anything that might be considered incriminating—tools, maps, travel notes on Jabal al Lawz—under a rock by the truck. We played it cool. We were on *their* turf, after all, and they had the gun. With nothing to lose, we cheerfully entered camp, all smiles and goodwill, pretending not to notice the carnage they'd made of our luggage. Larry extended another peace offering of water and candy bars, which they now hungrily accepted.

Pleasantries over, the four of us stood eyeing one another with deep suspicion. Out of ideas, we resorted to jokes and exaggerated hand signals (and a few awkward words of Arabic) to engage them in a short, tortured conversation. Their aggressive body language indicated they wanted to know who we were, where we were from, and where we were going. We flashed our passports and showed them our letter from the Saudi prince; then, flying by the seats of our pants, we asked if they knew Ibraham Frich. I handed Frich's picture to the one with the rifle and, with no more cards to play, we began to retrieve our belongings and put them in the truck. We held our breaths to see their reaction.

Suddenly the drama ended as quickly as it had begun. They took Frich's picture, hopped in their truck, and drove away, just like that. No good-byes, no acknowledgment, nothing. To this day we don't know who they were or what they wanted. But we didn't waste time pondering the mystery.

Larry threw his pack in the back of the pickup and barked, "Let's get out of here!" In less than five minutes we were bouncing along the rutted dirt path out of the desert. It seemed we'd dodged another bullet. "Something—or Someone—is looking out for us," Larry declared. We unfolded our maps and, after a brief discussion, set a course for the Red Sea, where we hoped to find the Arabian landfall of the mysterious underwater land bridge we discovered in Egypt.

THE SPRINGS OF ELIM

From the beginning, as far back as Los Angeles when we sketched our first rough itinerary, the town of Al-Bad kept surfacing. It lay strategically between Jabal al Lawz and the Straits of Tiran, sitting dead center in a broad valley that seemed a likely Exodus route. Studying a succession of old maps, we noticed they all showed notations of ruins near Al-Bad. Flushed now with confidence, certain we'd already made the discovery of the millennium, Larry and I wanted to see what *these* ruins were all about.* If our theory were correct and the Israelites had indeed traveled the valley toward Mount Sinai, they would have passed through Al-Bad. As long as it was on our route to the coast, we figured it couldn't hurt to take a quick look around.

(We have since learned that Al-Bad is widely known in this corner of Saudi Arabia as the ancient city of Madyan [or

Midian], known throughout the Muslim world as the hometown of Jethro, Moses' father-in-law. According to Jewish scholar Allen Kerkeslager, contributor to the book *Pilgrimage and Holy Space in Late Antique Egypt* [Edited by David Frankfurter: Brill, Leiden, Boston, Koln, 1998], ancient Jewish traditions located Mount Sinai in northwestern Arabia near the city of Madyan long before theories of Hebrew pilgrimage to the southern Sinai Peninsula developed. He writes: "The evidence . . . demonstrates that traditions relating Mt. Sinai to the site of ancient Madyan at modern Al-Bad' extend at least to the time of the oldest portions of 250 B.C. In contrast, the earliest solid date for the appearance of traditions locating Mt. Sinai in the southern Sinai peninsula is ca. A.D. 350." Citing ancient Jewish historians like Josephus, Kerkeslager insists that in identifying the real Mount Sinai three considerations must be taken into account: 1) The mountain must be in northwestern Arabia; 2) The mountain must be near Al-Bad' [ancient Madyan]; and 3) The mountain must be the highest mountain in the surrounding region. Jabal al Lawz, clearly the tallest mountain in northwest Saudi Arabia, fits all three criteria.)

Corroborating Kerkeslager's research is an opinion offered by a leading Old Testament expert, Frank Moore Cross, Hancock Professor Emeritus of Hebrew and Oriental Languages at Harvard University. In his new book From Epic to Canon, Cross says he began to suspect Mount Sinai lay in Saudi Arabia after Hebrew archaeological surveys of the Sinai Peninsula turned up nothing. "The Israeli surveys of the Sinai have been intense," he writes, "and the lack of archaeological remains from this crucial period becomes a very strong argument (from silence) against the peninsula of Sinai as the area in which Sinai-Horeb and Qadesh were located."[1]

In light of these developments, Cross adds, "Israel's early contacts with Midian make sense. Sinai-Horeb must be sought in southern Edom or northern Midian (modern day Saudi Arabia). This view, long held by German scholars but rejected by most American and Israeli scholars, including the writer, now appears to be sound." He goes on to cite traditions passed down in Israel's archaic hymns as further evidence that the Exodus could not have culminated in the Sinai Peninsula. "Yahweh came from Teman," he writes, "Mt. Paran, Midian, and Cushan (the Song of Habakkuk); the Song of Deborah sings of Yahweh going forth from We'ir, marching forth from Edom; the Blessing of Moses states that Yahweh came from Sinai, beamed forth from Se'ir, shone from Mount Paran. These geographical designations cannot be moved west into the peninsula now call Sinai."

Cross was recently quoted by the Associated Press concerning the Feb. 26, 2000, pilgrimage by Pope John Paul II to the traditional site of Mount Sinai in the southern Sinai Peninsula. Suggesting the Pope might be worshiping at the wrong mountain, Cross asserted that the biblical Mount Sinai is most likely located in present-day Saudi Arabia. "A great many scholars are now coming around to the notion that Sinai is in fact in northern Arabia," said Cross, 78, noting that the Sinai Peninsula took its name from the tradition of the traditional mount's location, which cannot be dated any earlier than the fourth century.[2] He credited nineteenth-century German scholars with introducing the Saudi-Sinai theory, and said his own thinking changed after archaeological work in the Sinai

Peninsula during the Israeli occupation of 1967–1982 showed no signs of ancient habitation during the presumed time of Moses and the Exodus (see page 169).

The thirty-kilometer trip took approximately two hours—a welcome drive to collect our thoughts and nurse a host of aches and pains. The road to Al-Bad spanned a high plateau bisecting rugged mountain ranges whose arid buttes spawned occasional gnarled trees and sparse vegetation. As we approached Al-Bad, however, the austere, high desert turned suddenly into a lush, green valley brimming with tall, flowing palm trees. And *water*—lots of sparkling wells peeked up from compact, concrete reservoirs. It seemed we had run across a true oasis in a sea of baked earth.

"Are you registering with this?" I asked Larry, who shrugged. I reminded him that, according to the Bible, the Israelites camped at two prominent stop-off points after crossing the Red Sea. The first was a spring where the waters were too bitter to drink; the second was a rejuvenating oasis, just like this, located between the Desert of Shur and the Desert of Sin. Scripture refers to it as the springs at Elim, a palm-shaded rest stop where Moses and his parched countrymen found rest and refreshment. I parked the truck and strolled slowly beneath the cool, shaded canopy. It seemed to hold the unbearable heat at bay. Maybe it was my imagination, but the heat seemed not to penetrate—no wonder wandering nomads so cherish these rare, verdant sanctuaries. A network of primitive cisterns, burrowed at sand level and lined with cement to prevent seepage, pockmarked the oasis. I knelt down, cupped my hands for a sip—and tasted the sweetest water I'd ever known.

Larry followed suit, splashing his face and body like a playful otter, guzzling water with glee. One would have thought we were dying of thirst, though our truck still carried cases of water. Dripping wet, I walked to the truck and returned with my Bible, reciting for Larry a verse from Exodus 15:27: "Then they came to Elim, where there were twelve springs and seventy palm trees, and they camped there near the water." Elim lay near the home of Moses' father-in-law Jethro, who was said to live within a few days' walk of Mount Sinai. Standing in the shade of towering palm trees, I counted exactly twelve springs of water.

The sun bore down with a vengeance, making us hesitant to leave this comfortable retreat. The spring water revived our spirits, as did this startling find. *What an amazing land*, I mused, *where thirty-five-hundred-year-old treasures keep leaping out at us from the pages of history!* It was as if cryptic trail markers had been trapped in time, just waiting out the millennia for someone to connect the dots. Here again, a vivid picture emerged—this oasis lay a few days' walk from Mount Sinai, precisely where the Bible suggests it *should* be. With a twinge of sadness, we left the oasis and drove into Al-Bad, wondering if we'd refreshed ourselves at the very pools Moses enjoyed so long ago.

"MOSES WAS HERE!"

The town of Al-Bad isn't much more than a small village of dusty shanties and uneven rows of tents. With a population no larger than five hundred people, it still spreads out over a couple of square miles. On our map the ruins we sought appeared to lie due north of the town, but after circling the area for more than an hour, we figured to cut our losses and enlist the help of some locals. Language barriers aside, *someone* should be able to point us in the right direction. We parked along the main commercial block, then split up and went knocking on doors (or tent flaps, as the case may be). As usual, the language gap combined with our impeccable timing—we arrived right at Muslim siesta time—slowed our search to a crawl. Larry and I entered one shop after another, only to find the owners sprawled asleep on the floor. Then our luck changed.

At a small grocery where we were bartering unsuccessfully with the proprietor, a young, neatly dressed Arabian fellow approached and offered his assistance. "I couldn't help overhearing your English," he said. "Can I be of help?" He introduced himself as Massud and responded to our compliments about his impeccable English by explaining that he'd been reared and educated in Syria. When we declared we were trying to find the ruins noted on our map near Al-Bad, he nodded and calmly replied, "Oh, yes. The ruins you speak of are located about five kilometers north of town. They are the caves of Moses."

Our mouths dropped open. "The caves of *whom?*" we asked. Massud seemed genuinely surprised by our reaction. "You said the caves of *Moses?*" I repeated. "How do you know this?" With a wave of his hand, he said, "Everyone around here knows the Prophet Musa [or Moses] stayed and camped at the town of Al-Bad. It's part of this town's heritage."

"Let me get this straight," Larry said skeptically. "Caves of Moses . . . here?"

"Yes, it's well known," Massud replied. He explained he was working as a translator for a Saudi archaeologist who—of all the wild coincidences—happened to be excavating those very caves. What an eerie, incredible stroke of good fortune, bumping into this walking tourist brochure for the ruins we needed to see!

Larry turned and asked me, "Does the Bible make any mention of caves where Moses lived?" I shook my head "no", to which Massud politely interjected, "The Prophet Musa has always been a part of this region's history. Moses' father-in-law, Jethro, pitched his tents near this oasis. In fact, we have found markings and writings in those caves that tell us Jethro and Moses' wife, Zipporah, were buried in tombs in the hillside. It is a heritage these people are very proud of."

Tombs? Markings? Moses, a local hero? Why would Moses, a Jewish prophet, be celebrated in a Muslim country? Massud seemed to grow impatient with our confusion. "Because Moses was a *Muslim* prophet as well," he said. "It's in all of our literature—Moses camped at the oasis of Al-Bad before moving on to Jabal al Lawz, the Mountain of Moses."

His last remark stopped us in our tracks. The Mountain of Moses? "You mean *Mount Sinai?*" I stammered. Our friend nodded, "Yes, Mount Sinai. It sits a short distance north of here."

The information crashed over us in waves, almost too much to absorb. Massud said it so casually, like saying, "There's a McDonald's on the corner." We hadn't expected this. It appeared the locals knew all along that Jabal al Lawz was Mount Sinai.

The plot just kept thickening. Now the question: How do we get to the caves? Larry and I were ready to rush off like two kids on a scavenger hunt, but Massud motioned for us to stop. "I urge you gentlemen," he warned. "Do not approach the caves. There are soldiers camped there now. It is fenced off and heavily guarded. It is forbidden." I was growing weary of all this talk of fences. Was there nothing of interest these people *didn't* throw a fence around? I think our friend sensed our determination and threw in another caution: "Please, *I urge you*, don't take a foolish chance."

We acknowledged his warning, thanked him, then forced a wad of bills into his hands as a token of appreciation. Turning to leave, I said, "Please, forgive our persistence, but—how exactly *would* one (if one were so foolishly inclined) go about finding these so-called caves?" At first Massud wouldn't budge, unwilling to be party to our imminent arrest. Finally, however, either because of our relentless prodding or feeling obligated by our generous gift, he relented and nervously directed us toward the ruins. Directions in hand, we thanked him again, then almost tripped over each other running to the truck. If Moses had indeed lived nearby, nothing would keep us from seeing the evidence.

Eleven

THE CAVES OF MOSES

> Jethro, Moses' father-in-law, together with Moses' sons and wife, came to him in the desert, where he was camped near the mountain of God. Jethro had sent word to him, "I, your father-in-law Jethro, am coming to you with your wife and her two sons" (Exod. 18:5–6).

A lone sentry exited the guardhouse, faced Mecca, and knelt for afternoon prayers. We watched from behind a small dune fifty yards away. Larry whispered: "If he's the only one, we shouldn't have too much trouble slipping under the fence once it gets dark. We'll just wait until he's asleep."

The caves lay a quarter mile beyond the guardhouse, just inside a steel-mesh fence topped with rows of barbed wire. From a distance the caves looked like a fossilized honeycomb, or a petrified hump of Swiss cheese, embossed into the rolling, sloping, straw-colored land. Dozens of them lay exactly where Massud had said: two kilometers south of Al-Bad.

"They're a little underwhelming, wouldn't you say?" I whispered to Larry. "Not much more than small, dark holes in the hillside." Larry didn't answer but continued to scan the dimpled bluffs with his binoculars. I had a hard time picturing the heroic Moses rearing his family here. Would God's prophet hole up in these cramped caves those forty years of exile, tending Jethro's sheep? If it were true, then he had indeed spent his middle years in utter obscurity. Had he occupied these dank caves, herding sheep, he would indeed have been the lowest of the low—a condition which somehow fit. Only a mighty God could have raised Moses from such humble depths to become a prophet able to humble Pharaoh! Only God could've forged a cave-dwelling shepherd into the framer of a mighty nation.

From our dune we spied a number of spots where it would be easy to slip under the fence after dark. The guards would be asleep, and we'd be in and out in less than an hour. It seemed feasible. We returned to the pickup and followed the dirt road as it curled away from the guardhouse and ambled toward the far end of the compound. I drove slowly, looking for another portal, some section of fence where we might infiltrate the compound with less risk. Instead, we found big trouble.

Crowning a low rise half a mile from the caves, I steered the Datsun slowly around a bulging rock outcropping—only to gape into the maw of a full-fledged army brigade. Our truck faced the fence, unannounced and in full view of at least a hundred soldiers marching in full combat gear, all armed with submachine guns. Further into the complex we saw construction workers excavating the area, moving dirt and kicking up clouds of dust. "This is what Massud was talking about," Larry gasped. "Let's get out of here!" I cranked the truck into reverse and punched the gas, peeling backwards over the ridge and out of sight. "I don't think they saw us," I said. Nonetheless it chilled our plans to sneak into the caves.

We drove back to the smaller guardhouse; the sentry had evidently finished his prayers and gone back inside. We parked the truck out of sight and returned to our lonely dune to snap a few photos of what could be our only look at the caves. On the other side of the wadi, some two hundred yards from the caves, lay a separate compound, fenced in like the caves but much larger. It contained ruins resembling a crumbling adobe pueblo, more the size of a bustling village than an isolated encampment—clearly another major archaeological site. "Maybe that's where Jethro lived," said Larry. "Maybe Moses slept in the caves while Jethro (the priest of Midian) enjoyed the high-end, adobe condos."

As we stood chuckling, admiring the caves and ruins, a car pulled up and parked forty feet away. Before we could hide our cameras, out stepped a short, stocky fellow, who marched over and introduced himself with an unmistakable Scottish brogue. Our new acquaintance informed us that he was a minister from Scotland. He seemed eager to chat. While it felt good to see a friendly face, it seemed equally odd, in our undercover mode, to talk openly to what amounted to an English-speaking "tourist." The Scot took note of our cameras and warned, "You'd better not be seen with those around here, lads." Then, grinning, he reached into his vest pocket and pulled out a tiny automatic and began shooting quick bursts of film of the caves. Larry and I gave each other a look that said, "Who *is* this guy?"

Whoever he was, he told us, "I'm also a pastor doing some research. Those caves over there—they're the caves of Moses!"

"Yes, we know," I said, but before we could ask another question, the Scot popped his camera back in his pocket, bid us a cheery farewell, and drove off. "Take caution, lads," he yelled as his car vanished into the dust.

Perplexed, Larry and I lingered to decide our next move. "If there *are* petroglyphs in those caves that prove Moses had been here," he said slowly, "then why wouldn't the Saudi government release that information? It would be a crowning archaeological discovery." But we both knew why. The political and religious tensions between Israel and Saudi Arabia would forever keep the contents of those caves, and the truth about Jabal al Lawz and ancient Midian, a carefully guarded secret.

We wrestled with all the pros and cons, brainstorming every possible scenario for reaching those caves, before deciding against a nighttime incursion. With so many soldiers milling about, it was just too risky. We had been lucky so far. And we'd already bagged our real trophy—Mount Sinai. No sense getting shot now. As badly as we wanted a look in those caves, we chose to move on. After a final, longing gaze, we returned to the truck and drove east toward the coast.

BITTER SPRINGS

> Then Moses led Israel from the Red Sea and they went
> into the Desert of Shur. For three days they traveled in
> the desert without finding water. When they came to
> Marah, they could not drink its water because it was
> bitter. . . . Then Moses cried out to the LORD, and the
> LORD showed him a piece of wood. He threw it into the
> water, and the water became sweet (Exod. 15:22–25).

105

Λ

We set our sights on Ra's ash Shaykh Humayd, a small island
connecting the Straits of Tiran to the Saudi mainland. On our
map, Ra's ash Shaykh Humayd was the spot where we expected
to find the eastern tip of the underwater land bridge. This little nub is also called Tiran Island, and according to
nineteenth-century explorer Sir Richard Burton, it was once
called "Pharaoh's Island." "Maybe Pharaoh's chariots washed
ashore there," Larry quipped, a remark that probably hit closer
to the truth than we realized. Of one thing we felt certain—we
were now tracking the Exodus route *backward* through Midian
to the Red Sea.

The only road between Al-Bad and Tiran Island is a reasonably
well-maintained one-lane, asphalt turnpike that cuts through a
broad, open-ended valley. This natural byway would have
offered the Israelites a logical passage on their northward trek
to the mountain. The look and feel of the topography gave us
good reason to expect at least one more tantalizing find. I'd
already alerted Larry that the Hebrews stopped at two historic
places on their pilgrimage to Mount Sinai—the first one being
the bitter springs of Marah, located three days inland from the
Red Sea.

Leaving Al-Bad, we reset the odometer to zero. Scripture says that after crossing the Red Sea, the Israelites traveled for three days without finding water, and "when they came to Marah, they could not drink its water because it was bitter" (Exod. 15:22). In three days the Israelites would have been able to travel on foot approximately thirty kilometers, or ten kilometers per day. Since we knew exactly how far we were from the coast, it was easy to calculate where we might intersect the springs of Marah: approximately twenty kilometers south of Al-Bad. With one eye on the odometer, we began scouring the plain with our binoculars for some sign of a spring, lake, or reservoir. At twenty kilometers, nothing appeared. We drove another five kilometers, then ten, driving slowly to survey the parched tableau—still nothing.

Then, just as we were about to turn around, large, dry, mud-caked flats appeared in the distance. It looked to be the remnant of an enormous, dead lake. On closer inspection, it was actually *several* dry basins spanning dozens of square miles, each one varying in size from a large lake bed to something smaller than a fishing pond. It was all concentrated into a chalky, low-lying depression, or what looked to be a vast water collection point during wet seasons. I parked the truck on a small palisade near the plain and stood for a moment, trying to appraise these sun-cracked, alkaline flats. Our odometer put us at precisely three days, travel by foot from the Straits of Tiran.

Scattered across the plain and poking up like giant anthills (or miniature volcanoes) we saw scores of smooth-faced, alkali-encrusted mounds, some standing as high as three feet. Hiking down to inspect, we saw they were in fact primitive wells, formed of packed, piled mud—some shallow, others as deep as eight feet, all with interior walls scarred and grooved from ropes used over the ages to raise and lower buckets. I dipped a finger into a shallow well and touched it to my tongue. *Achh!* One vile, caustic drop made my teeth ache. Unless these Bedouins had cast-iron stomachs, I doubted they'd ever dare drink it. "They probably water their sheep with it," Larry suggested. He knew from his Montana youth that sheep thrive on hard, alkaline water known to sicken other livestock.

I examined a few more wells, while Larry strolled over to a stand of spindly looking trees, perched like hairbrush bristles against a vacant horizon. "Hey, look," he called out—"Wood!" I shrugged as if to say, "So what?" He broke off a twig and held it up. "You know," he said, "for the bitter water." Smiling proudly, Larry was at last getting the hang of this biblical detective work. He had read the verse: "Then Moses cried out to the LORD, and the LORD showed him a piece of wood. He threw it into the water, and the water became sweet" (Exod. 15:25).

"Ahhh," I replied, nodding broadly so he could see me. "Wood!" Maybe the locals drank this rancid water after all. Maybe they just tossed a stick in there, like Moses. Maybe the scrawny trees had some Ph-neutralizing properties. Who's to say? But by this stage of the journey, nothing would've surprised me.

As with everything else, there is no way for us to *prove* these are the waters of Marah memorialized in Exodus. Yet like every other find we had documented, this one served as its own defense. The basin was definitely large enough to accommodate the Hebrew multitude, while its distance from the Straits of Tiran (approximately 35 kilometers) coincided closely with the Israelites' three-day walk from the Red Sea. Finally, the water's unrivaled bitterness fit the narrative to a tee. As we read from the Bible and projected ourselves into the biblical scene, we felt sure these had to be the springs of Marah. We crossed it off our growing list of stations of the Exodus, another cheering development.

Yet our zeal was tempered by a wasting fatigue that had been building for the past two days. Stress, heat, and an almost total absence of sleep had taken their toll. We drove on in a mental fog, longing to reach Ra's ash Shaykh Humayd before dark. When we finally arrived at the Straits of Tiran, a beautiful, peach-blossom sunset blanketed the sky above the most charming stretch of beach I'd ever seen.

THOUGHTS OF HOME

What a strange, mystical experience to gaze across the Straits of Tiran *into* Egypt. Not so long ago, I'd sat aboard the *Fantasea*, tingling with wonder at what lay on the other side of the underwater land bridge. Now we were there, staring at the eastern tip of that same submerged reef. Watching it snake through the surf and tagging shore not fifty yards from our camp was like finding the end of the rainbow for us. A circle had been completed that filled me with an indescribable sense of accomplishment—a fullness, a significance I'd never known.

As our journey neared its end, my heart soared. Sore, tired, and filthy, we rejoiced at our imminent return to civilization. We hadn't bathed since the Tabuk Sahara, and the grease and grit from days of climbing mountains, eating dust, and sweating off pounds of flesh in the furnace heat, hung on us like fish scales. Mercifully, Ra's ash Shaykh Humayd turned out to be an almost unearthly delight, the perfect spa at which to mend and recuperate. Its charming strip of pebbled beach framed a secluded cove of marbled blue waters, as beautiful a beach as can be found at any of the world's exclusive resorts. And we had it to ourselves! Within minutes of our arrival, we stripped to our trunks and raced into the looking-glass lagoon. Nothing ever felt so good as sudsing up and scrubbing off our layers of scum in the cool, salty surf.

Drying off in the baking sun, we realized how badly we had sun-burned. The fierce sun even had scorched pinpricks through the weave of my watchband, leaving my wrist tattooed with tiny red welts. Larry's face and nose looked the hue and texture of sun-dried tomatoes. Yet they seemed minor battle scars next to the personal triumph that enrobed us. We built a lovely fire, dined on dehydrated beef Stroganoff, and settled down for the night, braced by the sense we were probably the first men since Moses to retrace the entire Exodus route.

A day before we had climbed the tallest mountain in Midian, where Moses completed *his* mission. Now we had descended to the very spot where the Israelites likely emerged from the Red Sea. It didn't seem possible—a thought that only intensified our euphoria. For those few moments, I even deluded myself into thinking that God was well pleased with our efforts.

UNFINISHED BUSINESS

As the fire died, I stared silently at the gulf. I could see all the way to Egypt, where the thin, circling strobe of a lighthouse marked the spot where months earlier we had first conceived of this adventure. Seeing it from such a distance somehow reminded me how homesick I had grown. It seemed we had been on this journey for months. And it felt longer than that since I'd hugged my family.

On the hill above us, lights from a mosque winked down on the waters. Further up the shoreline, nestled into a sandy ridge, glowered the dark shadow of a military pillbox—a bunker, no doubt, left from the Six Days War. I'd had my fill of Saudi Arabia. I was weary of all the secrecy, frustrated by the language barrier, stressed out by the ever-present threat of exposure and arrest. I was sick of the heat, sick of the dust, sick of the desert. I was sick of the kingdom, period! I had been here only a week, but if I *never* returned to this blistering, dust-caked desert of a country, it would be too soon.

At that moment my thoughts turned toward the wandering Hebrews and a terrible sadness came over me. Once they stood on this beautiful beach on a day of worship and rejoicing. God had just delivered them from Pharaoh's grasp. They had just witnessed the miracle of the ages, walking triumphantly through the midst of the Red Sea to new freedom, to a new beginning.

"I will sing to the LORD,
    for he is highly exalted," they sang to the heavens.

"The surging waters stood firm like a wall;
    the deep waters congealed in the heart of the sea . . .

In your unfailing love you will lead
    the people you have redeemed.
In your strength you will guide them
    to your holy dwelling" (Exod. 15:1, 8, 13).

It was to be their sweetest moment. Without knowing it, forty years of bitterness, brutal hardship, and war lay ahead.

Lying on the beach, staring out at the waves, I knew what awaited them. We'd just been through it: bitter springs, endless desert, indescribable heat. They would endure strife and dissension; families would tear themselves apart; they would face continual attack from fierce tribes and taste the futility of walking circles in a blistering desert; they would see their most stalwart warriors struck down, the hearts of their bravest men turned to wax. Before them lay a dream of a Promised Land— but most would never see it. Their bodies would lie scattered in the dust before their children embarked on the promised new life. What awful drudgery it must have been to languish those forty years in these bitter badlands!

Unlike God's ancient children, *we* could go home satisfied. We had accomplished what we set out to do. I could almost smell the crisp, cool Colorado mountain air. I was ready to leave.

†WELVE

UNFINISHED BUSINESS

We clattered down the highway toward Tabuk. Our Datsun was falling apart bolt by bolt. It seemed as if every strut, screw, and rivet holding it together was shaking loose. We half expected it to disintegrate at the next bump or pothole. Three shock absorbers ground and squeaked on their pins; one had snapped off altogether and now scraped the ground with a metal-on-asphalt screech. Both the brakes and the power steering were nearly gone. All four tires and rims wobbled on their axles, cartoonlike, as we bounced along. Driving the battered truck felt like wrestling a steer.

Larry and I weren't in much better shape. My back felt on fire again. Too many nights sleeping on the Datsun's narrow bench seat, too many days bouncing along in this pogo stick of a truck caused the disk to flare up. Larry sat quietly nursing his own collection of cuts, scrapes, and contusions. To top it off, we were out of both water and food. All I could think of was getting back to the Tabuk Sahara, ordering a nice room-service dinner, falling asleep on a king-sized bed, and booking our flight home.

Crumpled against the passenger door, Larry looked the picture of exhaustion. He seemed to be either sleeping or deep in thought, and I took it for granted he was as eager as I to get home. A mile or two ahead lay the dirt turnoff we had used to reach Jabal al Lawz. I thought, *Oh Lord, thank you that we don't have to take that road again.* Suddenly Larry piped up: "Hey, Bob, I've been thinking—we should go back to the mountain and see what's inside that fence!"

"WHAT?" I jerked my head around and looked at Larry as if he were out of his mind. "Yeah, ha, ha. You're kidding . . . *right?*"

If he were serious, then I was riding with a stranger, a man about whom I knew nothing save the streak of bald-faced machismo that seemed to guide his every move. Our truck was about to expire—*I* was about to expire, barely able to sit up. We both looked as if we had just washed ashore from a shipwreck. We got what we came for. Our job was finished. What could possibly be accomplished by returning to Jabal al Lawz, except maybe getting arrested and shot? Again I asked, "You're kidding, right?"

He wasn't.

"I just think we're being premature," he said hesitantly. "I mean, are we fooling ourselves? Sure, we found all these incredible landmarks—but did we really get all the evidence we need to prove our case? Would our findings hold up in a court of law?"

114

I said nothing.

He continued, trying to cast doubt on the quality of our pictures. "All I'm saying is, I think we need more. We took some of those shots from quite a distance. I'm not sure they're going to turn out."

I couldn't believe what I was hearing. But Larry was on a roll. "I also think we need to get inside that fence, get a closer look at those pillars and altars. Get a look inside the cave of Elijah."

I kept driving, jaw clenched, eyes glued to the road. "Larry," I said as calmly and diplomatically as I could manage, "You're being irrational. Quit worrying. We're fine. Our photos are going to be great. We have more than enough evidence."

In deathly silence we both stared out the cracked windshield, until I added a final point: "Larry . . . listen. Let's be reasonable. This truck's barely going to make it back to Tabuk, much less through that obstacle course of a desert. I'm a mess, you're a mess. We're out of food and water. I need to get home—I'm *needed* at home. So, just relax. You'll see, we'll be fine."

I finally prevailed, as much because I was driving and not Larry. I passed the turnoff without a second glance. Larry leaned back against the passenger side door and remained quiet until we checked into our hotel. It didn't concern me. I figured the heat had temporarily fogged his thinking. Now that we were back in the comfort of our room, I felt sure he would be relieved I had cast the dissenting vote. An uncomfortable way to end our adventure? Perhaps. But I was just glad we were finally on our way home. I couldn't have been happier.

BACK IN THE STATES

"Bob, bad news." It was Larry on the phone. We had been back in the States for a week, and I couldn't avoid the truth any longer. We had rushed our film to the processors and even arranged for geologists to look at our rock samples. The minute we had collected our photos, compiled all of our data, and revisited our conclusions, we shared the pictures—and our adventure—with close family and friends. I truly believed we had a fail-safe presentation. But if Larry's experience was anything like mine, we were in trouble.

"Bob," he said, "they're not buying it. I can see it in their eyes. Everyone's very polite; they say it's very interesting and all, but . . . I guess I expected them to do cartwheels."

Larry never once said, "I told you so," but it was clear his doubts about our evidence had been well-founded. People just weren't buying our story. Those with whom I'd shared our experiences also acted wonderfully polite and showed curiosity about our pictures and our theories behind them. But in general they responded to my slides and photos with some version of, "That's pretty interesting, but I don't know. . . ." And if this was the response of friends and family, what kind of sympathy could we expect to receive in academic circles?

I hated to admit it, but Larry had been right. We needed more evidence, more and better pictures. Many of our photographs had been taken from at least a mile away. Even with our powerful telephoto lens, the altars and pillars in our pictures looked like so many toothpicks and Tinkertoys. Our photos failed to capture the vastness and scope, much less the feeling, of the sites. They simply didn't do our adventure justice.

Larry and I were suddenly indignant. Who were these scoffers to call themselves our friends? Didn't they understand the risks we'd taken? They hadn't been with us in Egypt, on the Sinai Peninsula. Where were they when our truck got stuck in the sand? It had been a huge risk simply to leave the kingdom with this film and our rock samples. Didn't they understand that others had been arrested and jailed when they tried to leave? That could've been us.

Thankfully, we'd exited the kingdom with little resistance. Sure, there were long, nerve-wracking lines at customs. But none of our nightmares had come true. At the Tabuk Sahara we had wrapped all of our film and rock samples in enough layers of filthy socks and dirty underwear to discourage any customs agent. My worst moment occurred at the international terminal in Jedda. A customs agent, poking through my bags with a long stick, found my dog-eared leather Bible. He began thumbing through, then turned purposefully to the New Testament. He noted the first pages of the Book of Matthew, then closed the Bible. He looked at me with a sour smile. "I can see you're not Jewish," he said. "You can go."

Larry's scare came in the same customs line. He forgot the name of our fake Saudi sponsor and had to wing it on the exit questionnaire. But these proved minor interruptions. In general we passed through like clockwork. We nearly jumped for joy to hear the comforting sound of the stamp authorizing our visa documents.

Now it seemed as if it were all for nothing.

"Bob," Larry reminded me, "if we can't convince our friends and family, then we have a big problem." He declined to chastise me for refusing to return to the mountain when we had the chance, but now he issued a challenge. "What's behind that fence, Bob?" he asked. "What are they hiding? Let's go see what's back there. If we really believe that mountain is Mount Sinai, then we need to get behind that fence. If you and I don't do it now, it'll gnaw on us the rest of our lives."

He needn't have said it. I was already convinced. I really believed we had found Mount Sinai. But if no one else believed it, what did it matter? Larry would again foot the bill; already he had begun the visa process. So I said, "OK, I'll go back. But this time let's do it right!"

Thirteen

BEHIND THE FENCE

Less than two weeks after we first scouted the
blistering plains around Jabal al Lawz, we
found ourselves back in the kingdom. Once I
embraced the idea we had to return, I poured
myself into a whirlwind schedule of preparation and planning. This time, however, our
visas posed no problem. The Saudi prince had
returned and promptly provided a letter of
sponsorship. Using his London contacts, Larry
fast-tracked all our paperwork—legally—
through the Saudi embassy. It seemed we had
barely returned to the States when we were
back on a plane to Jedda, then Tabuk, where
we touched down shortly after sunrise. We
didn't bother with a hotel but immediately
rented a truck, bought our supplies, and drove
straight to the mountain.

This time there were no miscues, no getting
stuck. We knew the way, knew what we
needed, and knew what to expect. We cruised
past the sand pit where I injured my back two
weeks earlier and arrived at the mountain by

late afternoon. Rather than approaching the mountain's exposed backside as before, though, we drove straight to its east face—the portion protected by fence—staying low and out of sight by driving in a low-lying depression to a crescent-shaped stand of rocks. About a quarter mile across the valley from the altar of the golden calf, we hunkered down in the wadi, just out of sight of the guardhouse, and waited for dark.

To minimize the risk of being spotted, we planned a nighttime incursion. To this end we had purchased a pair of expensive, infrared, night-vision binoculars in London. As the sun set, we cooked a quick dinner on the truck's radiator and lay down in the sand. We hoped for a couple of hours sleep before our ascent. The stress and furious pace of our travel schedule— combined with fatigue from the first trip—had caught up with us.

But sleep was impossible. We knew what lay ahead. It would be a rigorous, high-risk operation. Climbing the craggy, scree-covered slope at night would pose many more problems than a daytime assault. Other obstacles also confronted us. We had to contend with a half-dozen Bedouin camps scattered about the base of the mountain. We could hear their bleating sheep, barking dogs, and see their campfires flickering across the valley floor. And at least two armed sentries guarded the base of the peak. We couldn't figure out why, in two short weeks, the peak had become such a popular gathering spot. But their presence significantly raised the stakes. I lay there wide awake, listening to the breeze, staring at the black-crested peak—both beautiful and menacing under the strobe-like moon. At 10:30 P.M., Larry rolled over and said, "I can't sleep. Let's just do it."

↓ Cornuke met Larry Williams (left), a commodities trader and former politician, during the search for Pharaoh's chariots in the Red Sea.

↑ A former SWAT team member and police investigator, Bob Cornuke, found the Bible to be a step-by-step road map to the stages of the Exodus.

↑ St. Catherine's Monastery, near the traditional Mount Sinai in the southern Sinai Peninsula. Thousands of tourists flock to the popular tourist attraction each year to pay homage at the site near where they believe Moses received the Ten Commandments. *Photo by Bob Cornuke*.

← The traditional Mount Sinai in Egypt's Sinai Peninsula. Archaeologists spent years surveying the mountain for evidence of the Exodus, and found nothing. *Photo by Bob Cornuke.*

↑ Apollo 15 astronaut (and the eighth man to walk on the moon) Jim Irwin (left) with Bob Cornuke on the summit of the traditional site of Mt. Sinai near St. Catherine's Monastery. After thoroughly inspecting the mountain, they concluded there was no evidence to indicate it was the biblical Mount Sinai described in the Old Testament.

↑ *"Was it not you who dried up the sea, the waters of the great deep, who made a road in the depths of the sea so that the redeemed might cross over?"* The mysterious underwater reef as seen from above, is the physical embodiment of the "road in the depths" described in Isaiah 51:10. Believed by the authors to be the actual Red Sea crossing spot, the sliver of ghost-white reef is a strategically placed land mass that might have allowed the Hebrew multitude to cross the deep abyss of the Gulf of Aqaba. *Photo by Bob Cornuke.*

↑ It is believed that water levels in the Red Sea have dropped through the millennia. Though heavy tides have eroded it through the years, plenty of the underwater reef remains to strand the occasional cargo ship (seen here) nearly a mile from shore. *Photo by Bob Cornuke.*

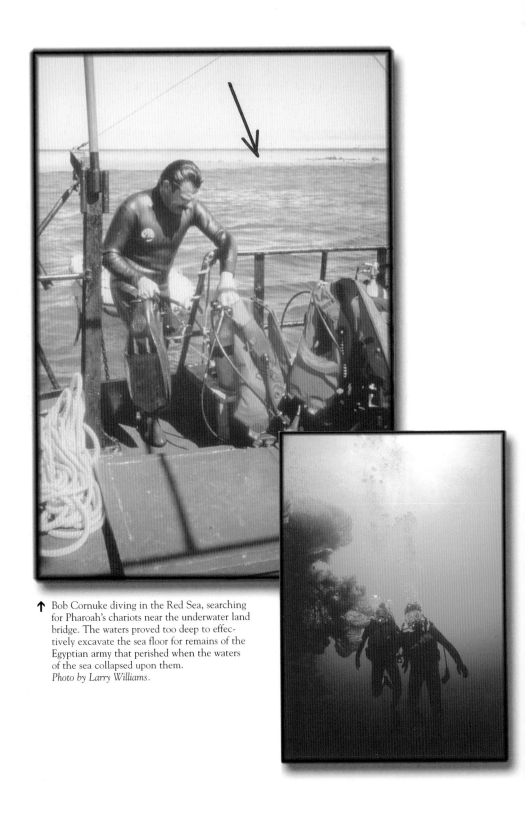

↑ Bob Cornuke diving in the Red Sea, searching for Pharoah's chariots near the underwater land bridge. The waters proved too deep to effectively excavate the sea floor for remains of the Egyptian army that perished when the waters of the sea collapsed upon them.
Photo by Larry Williams.

↑ *"Mount Sinai was covered with smoke, because the Lord descended on it in fire. The smoke billowed up from it like smoke from a furnace, the whole mountain trembled violently"* (Exod. 19:18–19). From a distance, the summit of Jabal al Lawz appears to be cloaked in a shadow, though the sky is clear and cloudless. On closer inspection, the duo found the peak's summit to be scorched black. *Photo by Bob Cornuke.*

← Bob and Larry Williams scuba diving in the Red Sea, inspecting the underwater land bridge. Located at the eastern arm of the Red Sea at the Straits of Tiran, the land bridge connects the Sinai Peninsula with Saudi Arabia, and sits precisely where a close reading of the Bible indicates the Israelites crossed over.

↑ *"And Aaron answered them, 'Take off the gold earrings . . . He took what they handed him and made it into an idol cast in the shape of a calf, fashioning it with a tool . . . He built an altar in front of the calf . . ."* Near the base of Jabal al Lawz, a quarter of a mile into the plain, Cornuke stumbled upon a huge altar of stacked granite. It was flat on top, and would have taken a large, experienced work force to lift into place. It was fenced off by the Saudi government as a forbidden archaeological site. *Photo by Bob Cornuke.*

↑ Etched on the altar were distinct shapes of cows and bulls resembling the Egyptian Hathor and Apis bull gods. Cattle have never been a domesticated livestock in Saudi Arabia, which raises the question: why would cattle be memorialized in stone unless they were driven there by the Israelites? *Photo by Bob Cornuke.*

↑ Reaching the summit of Jabal al Lawz, the duo found the dirt and rocks were burnt black and shiny, like melted black plastic. Clearly something unnatural, intensely hot, had incinerated the mountaintop. *Photo by Bob Cornuke.*

↑ Assuming the mountain to be volcanic, Cornuke broke one rock in half, revealing an inner core of plain brown granite. What type of heat could melt the surface rock to a black marble glaze, and leave the underlying granite intact? Exodus 24:17 states that the glory of the Lord was "like a consuming fire on top of the mountain." *Photo by Bob Cornuke.*

↑ *"Take in your hand the staff with which you struck the Nile, and go. I will stand there before you by the rock at Horeb. Strike the rock, and water will come out of it for the people to drink"* (Exod. 17:5–6). On the slope of Jabal al Lawz stood a towering pillar of rock, split laser-fine down the middle, approximately 20 inches wide from top to bottom. Was this the split rock at Horeb? Jim and Penny Caldwell, Americans working in Saudi Arabia in recent years, took this picture and others during several pilgimages they took to the mountain. We want to thank them for providing us some great photos for the book. *Photo by Jim and Penny Caldwell.*

← *"When he struck the rock, water gushed out, and streams flowed abundantly"* (Ps. 78:20). Water erosion at the base of the split rock. When Moses struck the rock the water, it would have erupted like a great geyser, creating deep furrows of erosion like these seen in the granite at the base of the split rock. *Photo by Jim and Penny Caldwell.*

← *"He brought streams out of the rocky crag and made water flow down like rivers"* (Ps. 78:16). Deuteronomy 9:21 speaks of a "stream that flowed down the mountain," where Moses disposed of the crushed remains of the golden calf. These water-polished boulders lie in the natural stream bed that runs down from the split rock, an ancient watershed furnishing clear evidence of a fast-rushing stream, large enough to serve the Hebrew multitude.

↑ *"He (Elijah) traveled forty days and forty nights until he reached Horeb, the mountain of God. There he went into a cave and spent the night"* Just below the summit of Jabal al Lawz sits a sizeable cave—the cave of Elijah?—large enough for a man to stand up inside. There is no cave on the traditional Mount Sinai in the Sinai Peninsula, as Scripture requires. Note the large, sprawling plain at the base of the mountain that would have provided an ample campsite for the Hebrew multitude (a feature also missing from the peak at St. Catherine's Monastery). *Photo by Jim and Penny Caldwell.*

↑ In Exodus 19:12, God ordered Moses to "put limits for the people around the mountain and tell them, 'Be careful that you do not go up the mountain or touch the foot of it.'" Set about the base of Jabal al Lawz, arranged at 400-yard intervals, piles of sun-bleached rocks like these formed a perfect semicircle. Were the orderly arranged rocks the sacred markers—the work of Moses' own hands? *Photo by Bob Cornuke.*

"Moses . . . got up early the next morning and built an altar at the foot of the mountain and set up twelve stone pillars representing the twelve tribes of Israel" (Exod. 24:4). Sitting at the foot of the mountain was a huge, V-shaped altar, clearly man-made. Badly weathered in spots it appeared to be a place of worship, perhaps where burnt offerings were made. Jabal al Lawz seemed to be revealing itself as a shrine to Mosaic law and testament, a sand and granite memorial to the great Exodus. *Photo by Jim and Penny Caldwell.*

↑ Twelve-Pillar Altar Site, Close-up

↑ The V-shaped altar from ground level shows raised trenches that may have been used to hold animals prior to or during burnt offerings. Ancient ashes were found on the floor of the altar, and remnants of stone pillars are visible in the foreground. *Photo by Jim and Penny Caldwell.*

↑ *"Then they came to Elim, where there were twelve springs and seventy palm treees, and they camped there near the water" (Exodus 15:27).* Had the duo stumbled across the seventy palms of Elim? On the trail to Jabal al Lawz, precisely where the Bible suggests it should be, is a true oasis in the middle of the desert. Cornuke and Williams enjoyed the shade afforded there by a large grove of palms—an unfamiliar sight in Saudi Arabia but closely resembling Scripture's description of the oasis at Elim. *Photo by Bob Cornuke.*

← ". . . and (Moses) set up twelve stone pillars representing the twelve tribes of Israel." Strewn near the V-shaped altar, toppled over and broken in sections, lay the hewn stumps of stone pillars. Cornuke counted them and found twelve stumps—perhaps the remains of the pillars Moses erected to represent the twelve tribes of Israel? It was the sum of evidence located about the mountain that spoke to its authenticity as the real Mount Sinai.

↑ Scattered throughout the oasis were a network of primitive cisterns—exactly twelve, as Scripture describes. Lined with cement to prevent seepage, the springs contained the sweetest-tasting water Cornuke had ever tasted, leading the duo to believe they had stumbled across Elim's palm-shaded rest stop. Was this where Moses and his parched countrymen found rest and refreshment? *Photo by Bob Cornuke.*

↑ Caves of Moses? Not far from the oasis lay the town of Al-Bad, where local legend insists the Prophet Moses once pitched his tents. Two kilometers south of Al-Bad, honeycombed into the sandy hills, sat a cluster of caves. Local archaeologists say they contain ancient writings indicating Moses' father-in-law Jethro once lived there. *Photo by Bob Cornuke.*

↑ *"For three days they traveled in the desert without finding water. When they came to Marah, they could not drink its water because it was bitter"* (Exod. 15:22–23). Thirty-five kilometers east of the Straits of Tiran, three days' walk inland from the Red Sea crossing site, sat a vast, alkaline mud flats pocked with bitter springs, numerous enough to accomodate the Hebrew multitude. Were these the Springs of Marah? If so, it was as if thirty-five-hundred-year-old treasures kept leaping out at the explorers as from the pages of Scripture.

INTO THE BRINK

With a flat-blade knife strapped to my leg and two small bottles of water in my pack, I took a deep breath and replied, "What are we waiting for?" Our plan was simple: using the night-vision binoculars to pick our way across the quarter mile of exposed plain, we would make a beeline to the fence. If all went well, we'd dig under it and crawl to the safety of the rocks. That would put us within a hundred yards of the archaeological site—the array of pillars and the altar we'd seen from a distance. We counted it a mixed blessing that the moon was now so bright you could read a book by it. The Milky Way looked like a low-lying cloud, its white-hot tail stroking the peak's summit—a lamp to light our way but also a searchlight to betray us.

Towering before us in the moonlight, steeped in shadow, sat Jabal al Lawz. An eerie light covered the peak, lending the contours of rock and shrub a pearly translucence. Moving one step at a time, we crossed the valley in spurts; Larry led for fifty yards, then I'd take over. In the quiet we could easily hear the mushing sound of our footsteps in the sand. Approximately two hundred yards into the plain—when we became fully exposed in the flats—the dogs started barking. First one, then two, then from everywhere. The night erupted in an ear-splitting symphony of blood-curdling howls. "Oh my God," Larry whispered. "Do they smell us? Can they see us?" I pulled out my knife, fully expecting, at any second, to see shadows of dogs racing at us from the plain. Larry scrounged for a stick to use as a club.

We had learned something of this ferocious breed earlier in the day. Driving in from Tabuk, we stopped in the plain to get our bearings, when one of the mangy curs charged us from the bushes. I barely had enough time to roll up the window before it smashed its face against the glass, barking wildly, foaming at the mouth. "It wants to eat me right through the glass!" I shouted to Larry, who frantically locked the door. Astonished at the raw display of feral aggression, we sped away but retained that disturbing image the rest of the trip.

There was little doubt these dogs could smell us. Our only hope was that the Bedouins would think we were a rabbit or a fox and keep the pack tethered. We kept moving toward the fence, trying to block out the noise and shuffling on hands and knees to muffle the squish of our footsteps. Less than forty yards from the fence Larry's arm shot up. "Wait!" he whispered. "Someone is there." He raised his binoculars and saw the green dot of a lit cigarette dancing in the black. Someone, a guard, a shepherd, was smoking a cigarette by the fence.

It was bad news. Very bad. Digging under the fence now was out of the question. We'd have to resort to Plan B, a bleak alternative. We had no choice but to soft-shoe another mile north in the exposed plain, dodging sheep dogs and Bedouins in the dark, until we reached the end of the fence; from there we'd have to climb halfway up the peak and then descend, inside the fence. Instead of a quick penetration from ground level, snap a few pictures, and beat a hasty retreat to the truck, we now faced the demoralizing prospect of an all-nighter on the precarious slope.

THE CLIMB

Hen-scratching our way through the darkness, we never were sure if the next shadow was a bottomless crevasse or a shallow chuckhole. I kept worrying about stepping on a cobra or grabbing a sleeping asp. We chugged water and gushed sweat. Larry stayed glued to the night-vision binoculars, trying to keep us from tromping through shepherds' camps.

Well after midnight we finally skirted the fence and began our climb. It seemed almost a miracle that we hadn't been intercepted by dogs or Bedouins. Out of water thirty minutes back, however, we were already packing a ferocious thirst. But with no choice but to press on, we started climbing, hand over foot, debating every move, painstakingly traversing our way diagonally up the mountain.

It took us another two hours before we could look down on the altar site. By then the moon had shifted hues, bathing the mountain in surreal, aquamarine sparkles. The valley floor looked like a giant snowfield. A wind picked up, making us shiver in our sweat-soaked shirts. Soon it howled across the rock face, blowing dust and whipping our faces. We stood on a narrow, teetering ledge, exposed and vulnerable. I could just make out the guardhouse below; farther south the ghostly white outlines of the pillar stumps; and then the vague, arrowhead-shaped altar. Shielding my eyes from the stinging sand, I turned to Larry and asked, "What are we doing here?" I could see the moon's bluish reflection in his eyes, the sheen of sweat on his brow. He turned and grinned. "We're making history," he said.

RAPID-FIRE RECONNAISSANCE

What appeared so clear from above, however, turned out to be a confusing maze of ridges and trenches at ground level. It took us two false starts to find the pillars. Scratching around in the dark on all fours, we had to scramble back up the slope, make cross-sightings and recalibrate our position, then scuffle down over rocks and prickly bushes to the bottom. Communicating in whispers and hand signals, scurrying in and out of shadows between boulders, we tiptoed past the guardhouse and came upon a series of odd structures neither of us had anticipated—strange stone circles.

Each structure was comprised of three large rings, not unlike the outer bark of a colossal redwood, forming exterior walls two-and-a-half feet thick. They measured eighteen feet in diameter, spaced five feet apart—and there were exactly twelve of them. But they weren't pillars. They looked more like ceremonial platforms, or perhaps large cisterns. They lay at the bottom of the ancient riverbed we'd seen before, so perhaps they once served as water storage reservoirs for the Hebrew tribes. We took a few pictures, muffling the flash with our hands, and started looking for the altar site.

THE PILLARS AND THE V-SHAPED ALTAR

> Moses . . . got up early the next morning and built an altar at the foot of the mountain and set up twelve stone pillars representing the twelve tribes of Israel. Then he sent young Israelite men, and they offered burnt offerings and sacrificed young bulls as fellowship offerings to the LORD (Exod. 24:4–5).

Frequently exposed in bright moonlight, we took our time, moving methodically across the rocky terrain, using the shadows for cover. We finally located the pillar-stones, or column fragments, along a makeshift road some thirty yards from the V-shaped altar. Again, we found a dozen of them, smooth to the touch, hand chiseled, like polished marble. We knew from Exodus 24 that after receiving the Law, Moses got up early in the morning and "built an altar at the foot of the mountain and set up twelve stone pillars representing the twelve tribes of Israel." The bases of these pillars seemed to fit the configuration of those cited in Scripture—close to the altar, at the foot of the mountain. Were these fractured columns remnants of the twelve pillars erected by Moses? What else would pillar stumps, beautifully cut and crafted, be doing in such an isolated spot, so far from civilization? "It's like finding fine marble pillars in the Mojave Desert," Larry said. "Something like this doesn't get here just by accident." Their size alone—eighteen inches in diameter and twenty-two inches tall—made them a find of some consequence. With growing excitement, we took several close-up photos and moved on toward the altar.

The altar, seen from above, looked impressive; seen up close it took one's breath away. Located at the foot of the mountain, as noted in Exodus 24:4, and shaped like a giant V, it resembled an airliner, wings spread and ready for takeoff. We walked its entire length, marveling at this hand-constructed, stone creation standing at the base of a mountain, in the middle of a desert not known for stone altars. It appeared to serve as a foundation of some sort, a third of a football field in length. What was it? Scripture says the altar Moses built was used for "burnt offerings," a place where young bulls were sacrificed "as fellowship offerings to the LORD" (Exod. 24:5). From our vantage, it looked like a corral where animals could be penned and later used for sacrificial offerings.

After we thoroughly inspected the altar and captured it on film, we agreed it could be the altar described in Exodus. As we left, I noticed Larry staring back at it with a look of astonishment. As if seeing it for the first time, he said, "This is the altar Moses built—isn't it?"

LAST GRASP FOR ELIJAH'S CAVE

By 3:30 A.M. we could see Elijah's cave several hundreds yards above us, a moonlit hollow gouged into the craggy slope. "There's still time to reach Elijah's Cave," I said, looking up. The memory of our earlier failure still rankled us. Larry was game. "Here goes nothing," he replied. We slapped palms, took some deep breaths, and began the most dangerous climb of our lives. The ascent had become treacherous not merely because of the distorting angle and hue of moon shadow on rock, but because, in our flagging condition, we had to climb straight up through loose rock and talus. The night-vision binoculars did us no good—they worked only at a distance—and since no clear path existed, we simply had to muscle our way up through the scree and jagged overhangs. We had dehydrated to such a degree that we had stopped sweating, and our arms and legs felt like tree limbs.

We struggled on, however, and after nearly an hour made it to within seventy yards of the cave. Then, worming my way around a sheer rock face, I slipped on a wobbly ledge and started sliding backwards on my stomach. I clawed frantically for any handhold, but the loose gravel kept giving way. I slid faster and faster toward a blind drop-off, five stories deep. At the last second, as my legs dangled over the edge, Larry reached out and grabbed the shoulder of my vest. I scratched my way up and regained my footing, then stared at the plunging ravine below, spiraling off into blackness. Larry had saved my life.

We sat for several minutes, gasping for air. We both knew I had almost cashed in my chips. *What did we think we were doing?* The sun now crept over the horizon; soon we'd be climbing in broad daylight. Our legs felt like bags of wet concrete; we had nothing to drink; and nearly a hundred yards of dangerous cliff still stretched above us. We both knew it was over. We weren't going to make it to the cave.

We dusted ourselves off and started back down. We felt satisfied with the photos we'd taken; hadn't we accomplished our primary objective? We shook off our disappointment and began quietly to celebrate a successful mission. It felt good to start working *with* gravity again. We made good time to the bottom, found a safe exit—a hidden spot near the fence, concealed by a large rock formation—then caught our breath and scurried undetected across the valley floor to our truck. We gave silent thanks—the Bedouin shepherds and guards continued to sleep soundly in their tents.

When we reached the truck, I unlatched the tailgate, ripped open a box of water, and started guzzling. Soon we stood in mud puddles, water drenching our clothes. Still we drank—ravenous, joyously. By the time we'd sated ourselves, we felt as fat and swollen as engorged ticks. "Well," said Larry, splashing handfuls of water on his face and neck, "We did it again!"

"Yeah," I answered, still out of breath.

We threw our packs in the pickup, devoured some protein bars, and wedged our cramping bodies back in the truck. We had one last stop before we could rest: the battlefield of Rephidim.

Fourteen

PRISONERS IN THE KINGDOM

The Amalekites came and attacked the Israelites at Rephidim. Moses said to Joshua, "Choose some of our men and go out to fight the Amalekites. Tomorrow I will stand on top of the hill with the staff of God in my hands" (Exod. 17:8–9).

In hindsight, we should have fled the desert the minute we descended from Mount Sinai. All we had to do was stow away our cameras, toss some equipment in the pickup bed, and drive back to Tabuk. We'd seen and documented almost every feature we had targeted, and then some. But we hadn't yet explored one final leg of the Exodus, one last landmark we hoped to find. We were ready to leave the kingdom once and for all, but the detective in me wanted more evidence.

It seemed a minor piece of the puzzle, certainly not a make-or-break find. Yet it stood prominent in the Exodus saga, and if we couldn't find it, could we really leave satisfied that Jabal al Lawz was the real Mount Sinai? We had to try and find the battlefield of Rephidim. Since Scripture didn't ignore it, neither should we.

In Exodus 17, the Israelites, moving toward Mount Sinai from the springs at Elim, fought a bloody battle against a warrior tribe known as the Amalekites. The Amalekites attacked the Hebrews in the plain of Rephidim, where the Israelites were camped mere days from Mount Horeb: "So Joshua fought the Amalekites as Moses had ordered, and Moses, Aaron and Hur went to the top of the hill. As long as Moses held up his hands, the Israelites were winning, but whenever he lowered his hands, the Amalekites were winning. When Moses' hands grew tired, they took a stone and put it under him and he sat on it. Aaron and Hur held his hands up—one on one side, one on the other—so that his hands remained steady till sunset. So Joshua overcame the Amalekite army with the sword" (Exod. 17:10–13).

A formidable opponent once stood between the Hebrews and Mount Sinai. Given the size of the Jewish army—likely exceeding one hundred thousand warriors, combined with a comparable force of Amalekites—the Rephidim battlefield must be immense. (It was just the absence of such a battlefield site anywhere near Jebal Musa, at St. Catherine's Monastery, that helped to disqualify that peak in our earlier investigations.) In our initial ascent of Jabal al Lawz however, we noticed a large, sprawling plain lying due south. At that distance it appeared large and flat enough to be the Rephidim battlefield.

With our sights set on one last trophy, Larry and I packed the truck and drove south in search of the plain. We followed yet another wisp of a trail about a mile and a half south of Jabal al Lawz. It led us through a valley that opened dramatically into a huge, yawning plain. We knew the plain looked large, but this massive, high-desert plateau easily measured fifteen miles long and seven to ten miles wide. In the distance several large peaks loomed over the flats and near its center stood one very large mound. "One of those peaks could have been the hill Moses sat on during the battle with the Amalekites," said Larry, by now keenly aware of the biblical history.

The plain seemed to be a perfect, level battlefield with over-looking peaks, more than large enough to host the Israelites' melee with the Amalekites. I felt certain that with several more days we could have found some trace of a major battle—weapon fragments, or armor—buried in the hard-packed sand. But we had to keep moving. We scratched the battlefield off our list and drove farther south, imagining we were treading over the bones of Rephidim's slain.

We forged ahead in swirling gusts of dust, hoping, almost as an afterthought, to complete the last leg of the Exodus route: the fifty-mile stretch from the springs at Elim to Mount Sinai. It was a risk to think we could find the passage taken by the Israelites through the mountains to the plain at Rephidim. In modern times, to get from the seventy palms at Al-Bad (or Elim) to Jabal al Lawz, you take the highway—a circuitous route north and east around the range encompassing Mount Sinai—before dropping south and approaching the peak from the east, through the desert. So far, however, we hadn't spotted any pass that might have led the Israelites north from their oasis rest stop *through* the mountains to Mount Sinai. And as fate would have it, we wouldn't.

Within twenty minutes of leaving the battlefield site, we were zigzagging the dunes like city slickers looking for a herd—hopelessly lost. Moses had something on his journey that we didn't: a pillar of cloud and fire to show the way. He knew what path to take through the wilderness. But the desert offered no mercy to greenhorns like us. I'm now convinced we made every possible wrong turn. And out there, if you take one wrong turnoff or head down one wrong valley, it just leads to more and more poor choices. It's like realizing you're lost in a maze the size of Alabama. The desert swallows you whole.

Soon everything looks the same, and your mind starts playing tricks on you. In our disoriented state, our maps and compasses became useless. Finally, in sheer desperation, we tried to drive our two-wheel-drive Datsun up a steep slope, out of the valley to a height where we could get our bearings. No luck. We kept getting stuck and ended up more confused than before. Our charmed run of success appeared to have ended.

But why panic? We still had water and several cans of gas. And though the heat scalded us in our unventilated truck, our bodies had started to acclimate to the desert. If we could just find our way back to an asphalt road, we'd be fine. Besides, Bedouins crisscrossed these badlands all the time in the heat of the day; it only figured we'd cross paths with one of them sooner or later. We would simply ask directions.

After wandering in circles for three more hours, however, we began to worry. As each hour passed, we had less and less water; with each mile, less and less gas. And it seemed as if we were straying ever farther into the wilderness. "Man, Bob," Larry kept saying, "where *are* we?"

Finally, far in the distance, we saw a truck rumbling toward us along the two thin, rutted grooves in the sand that pass in these parts for roads. As the truck approached, we both slowed down, then carefully pulled alongside one another (whoever veers from the path first, gets stuck in the sand). We came face-to-face with a nervous Bedouin, his bulging eyes darting. He peered warily into our dirt-caked window, then sat back with an arm resting on the window, waiting for us to speak. I leaned out with a broad smile and blurted out, "Asphalt!" This startled the Bedouin, who became even more baffled when Larry bent over me, arms flapping, and yelping: "As-phalt! As-phalt!"

We waited, embarrassed by our poor communication skills, as the Bedouin pondered our plight. After several moments, his dark eyes seemed to brighten. It appeared that he understood. Putting his truck in gear, he waved for us to follow him, then took off through the sand. I whipped the truck around, steering a tight arc—careful not to stray into the shifting sand—and gunned the engine to catch up to the Bedouin's cloud of dust.

GRIM TIMES ON THE FRONTIER

We followed the Bedouin back to the place where this story began. He took us across miles of wasteland, through an enormous box canyon walled on either side by towering granite, to a small outpost in the middle of nothingness. We pulled up to a building that seemed little more than a shanty plugged into the side of a chalky ravine. At first the settlement looked to be a sort of way station, dominated by a wooden platform with large tanks of gas and water. People likely gathered here from

miles around to fill their trucks and conduct a cheerless desert
trade. But it was actually a little town, caked in dust and reek-
ing of mutton. Its weathered residents wore long robes and
wrapped their heads with checkered gutras, like the sand people from *Star Wars*. The whole place had an alien feel.

We never did figure out why the Bedouin brought us here. But
whether by design or accident, he led us straight to the guys
we'd been trying to avoid the entire trip: to the soldiers with
the guns. Maybe he thought the regional sheriff or local militia
could help us. Whatever his motives, we knew we were in trouble when, the moment we parked the truck, out from the depot
ran a half-a-dozen Bedouin riflemen in drab green fatigues,
brandishing rusty machine guns and turn-of-the-century long
rifles. It wasn't the friendly greeting we'd hoped for. Unnerved,
we hopped from the truck, smiling, hands extended, eager to
put them at ease. But as they approached the truck, a soldier
saw our camera sitting on the front seat. Before we had a
chance even to say "Marhaba," someone shouted, "Jew!" and
we found six guns aimed at our heads.

Standing statue stiff, scared to blink, I was shaken by the irrational anger I saw in their eyes. I scanned the gray, grit-covered
town for escape options. Directly ahead stood the town jail, or
police station, its corrugated tin roof covered with tiny rust
holes, large patches of whitewash peeling from its crumbling
mortar walls. Beyond it, crowded under one of those black,
desert umbrellas, lay a flock of impoverished-looking sheep,
tongues hanging out, their wool dirty and matted.

Like idiots we had stumbled upon the Frontier Forces, the rat patrol of the Saudi outback. What we feared most had come to pass. We had gotten ourselves lost—and under arrest.

Fifteen

THE PEACE OF GOD

The guards enjoyed sliding shells into their turn-of-the-century long rifles and pressing the loaded muzzles to our heads. The shells, odd sized and outdated, came from our captors' stiff, cracked leather bandoliers, worn loosely across the chest, like Mexican bandits. And their rifle butts, marred and stained black from decades of dirt and sweat, were barely recognizable as wood.

But we were quite sure everything worked.

I held my breath as a Bedouin nudged his battered rifle against my temple. He waited just long enough to see my jaw clench, then slowly pulled the trigger. *CLINK*! Peals of laughter filled the cell block. I didn't dare bat an eye. Then another guard strolled over to Larry, leaned in close, and screamed "*Jew*!" They thought we were Jewish spies or Jewish archaeologists sent to unmask the secrets of Moses. That explained their almost drunken rage: glazed eyes, spitting the word—*JEW*! If they truly thought us Jews, there would be no negotiations, no bargaining. We'd soon be dead.

The drill continued for nearly fifteen hours, the only break coming during the foul tea rite. Despite it all, I'd developed a fondness for the two Bedouin boys who graciously served us every quarter hour. Their cheerfulness and dutiful attention to our cups brought a ray of light amid the gloom.

138

Eventually the guardhouse commander grew visibly impatient. He kept pulling his old World War I-era pistol from his shoulder holster and checking the rounds. *What are they waiting for?* I wondered. If we are under arrest, what are the charges? Were they waiting for us to confess to something? So far as we knew, they hadn't yet searched our truck, where they would find ample evidence to charge us as spies. Perhaps they were just waiting for a specified time—after prayers, perhaps—to shoot us and be done with it? The look of disgust in the commander's eye told me that, if he had his way, we'd soon be standing before a firing squad.

That's when it hit me: it really didn't matter! *I was no longer afraid.* I didn't want to die, but dying here didn't frighten me. And it wasn't merely a fatalistic acceptance of my destiny. In the eye of this hurricane, I felt a genuine, inexplicable peace. *Peace?* The very concept seemed ludicrous under such circumstances. Yet there it was, a steady calm shielding me from anxiety. From what unexpected corner had this peace appeared?

In my mind's eye, the scene replayed itself, the definitive moment of my life. Standing on top of Mount Sinai, I could see the peak's black crown testifying to a terrible, otherworldly fire.

I could feel its slick, melted rocks—rocks that spoke of the devouring presence of an almighty God. A shiver ran down my back as I recalled the terror I'd felt at our trespass. What could compare to *that*? After seeing what I'd seen and standing where I'd stood, what did I have to fear?

Freeze-frame snapshots of the past two weeks clicked off in my mind, a complete portrait of our journey. I could see the cleft in the rocks, where God had revealed his glory to Moses; I recalled the massive altar of the golden calf, the split rock at Horeb, the ancient, water-polished riverbed. It was all there. I had seen them with my own eyes. The boundary markers in the plain . . . the pillars, the V-shaped altar . . . the cave of Elijah. Still they kept coming. The springs at Elim, where we'd quenched our thirst . . . the seventy palms, where we'd found shade . . . the bitter waters of Marah . . . the caves of Moses . . . the underwater land bridge. We'd seen it all, Larry and I. We'd *done* it—we had retraced the Exodus.

Peace? Yes, the memory of our exploits brought peace even in this den of ranting lunatics. Now they were heckling Larry, whose face flushed red and sallow at the same time, a palette of terror and despair. In what might be our final moments, I grieved for my friend. Yet even as I watched, a lightness filled my heart. My mind stirred awake, suddenly ablaze with thoughts of God! My lifelong fear of the abyss dissolved before the knowledge of God. Truth awoke within me on Mount Sinai, and faith entered in. Now the circle was complete. I *felt* it. From somewhere deep within, swelling like Elim's pools from the hard clay of my soul, gushed a torrent of—*faith!* A smile creased my lips; next it was all I could do to keep from laughing. I wanted to shout for the whole village to hear: My

God, you're alive! You're real! The Living Word, my Savior. I know it's you! Lord, forgive me for ever doubting.

Nothing brings a man into God's presence like being completely alone and vulnerable, with eternity staring him in the face. When all there is between you and infinity is faith, when there are no distractions, no job, no phone calls—when nothing else exists but you and God—that's when you discover true intimacy. I never felt more at peace than when I stared death in the face. I knew I was in God's presence. His Holy Spirit overshadowed me, called to me. As the guards goaded and prodded Larry with their rifles, I was lost in the sweetest, most trusting prayer I've ever known.

"Lord," I prayed, "I'm ready to come into your kingdom. If I die right now, right here in this jail cell, I'm ready. You have proven yourself to me. You showed me the Truth, and set me free. Though I lied and broke laws and trespassed to do it, you still allowed me to stand on your holy mountain. You spared me. You blessed me. You hid me in your cleft, so I could finally know—100 percent—that your Word is true, that you died for me. Lord, you paid the price for me—and I've accepted it cheaply most of my life. You carried my cross, but I've been living for myself. I've been a fraud, thinking I knew you. But I've just been going through the motions."

I paused and let these words settle into my heart. Then I continued: "I now ask your forgiveness. I repent of everything I've done to grieve you. I now want to pay the price for *you*, to carry *your* cross. Jesus, I'm ready to die and be with you. But this one thing I promise: if I get out of this, I no longer belong to myself. I'm yours completely. The knowledge of you excites my soul.

From this day forward, I am your servant to do with as you please."

My mind drifted back to our crisis. The soldiers still stood there with their guns, but my restlessness had vanished, along with my fear. Nothing remained but quiet surrender. Unburdened, released, I lay back against the mortar, closed my eyes, and fell asleep.

GUARDHOUSE PHYSICIANS TO THE RESCUE

A shout snapped me awake. Three feet away Larry weathered another verbal assault, but this time the guards seemed to be gearing up for more physical threats. One stood off to the side, rolling up his sleeves. Ignoring the guard's menacing advance, Larry craned his neck in my direction and whispered, "Bob, *listen*—we need a plan, or they're going to kill us."

"Do you have anything in mind?" I whispered back.

He paused, glanced at the guard, then from the side of his mouth said, "Pretend you're a doctor!"

"*What?*" I said. "How am I supposed to do *that?*"

"Don't worry about it," he replied. "These people are all sick. They trust doctors. Just stay calm and. . . ." He intentionally raised his voice and, pointing at me for all to see, said, "Tell them you're a doctor!"

The room went silent. The guards froze in place. The word *doctor* stopped them in their tracks. The whole garrison turned and faced me. *Uh-oh,* I thought. *What now?* Across the room, the

camp commander stood up and looked me over. "*Doctor?*" he
asked, holstering his pistol. Clearing a path through the other
guards, he walked toward me with a scowl, leaned over, and
pressed his face close to mine. Then he raised his hand as if to
punch me. I winced. *This is it*, I thought. *I'm dead.* I steeled
myself for an impact that never arrived. I raised my head to see
him pointing at his eye. He wanted me to treat his bloodshot,
watery eye! The guards, now completely engrossed in the
drama, put down their rifles. Everyone waited to see what the
"doctor" was going to do. I glanced at Larry, who sported a
tight, mischievous grin.

There was nothing to do now but play along. To pull it off, I
needed the medicine kit from the truck. A physician friend had
stocked it with all manner of pills, antibiotics, and ointments.
It sat under a tarp in the back of the pickup. Larry rose and,
motioning toward the truck, said, "Supplies! Supplies!" and
gestured as if he were wearing a stethoscope. A guard stuck a
rifle in his face and ordered him to sit down. I appealed to the
commander, pointed to his eye, then to the truck. He finally
agreed to let me go to the pickup with an armed escort. I
retrieved the bag, being careful not to reveal the truck's other
contents, and returned to the jail, where all the guards had
lined up behind the commander, as if in a waiting room. Each
nursed an assortment of boils, cuts, and internal ailments. The
peace I felt a few moments earlier now turned into a large knot
in my stomach.

The commander waited. I fumbled about, unfamiliar with the
kit's contents, rifled through the bag, and finally pulled up
handfuls of bottles, packs, and prescription drugs. Somehow, in
the middle of the mess, I grabbed a tiny bottle of Visine. Eye

drops! Hiding my surprise, I motioned for the commander to tilt his head back, then squeezed half the bottle in his eye. He blinked several times, and when he opened it a few seconds later, his eye turned white as a snowflake. The drops not only got the red out; they evidently soothed the pain as well. The commander smiled and stood with a grateful bow; in so doing, he anointed me the new guardhouse physician. Now everyone pressed in, pushing for a place in line. Women and children from the village wandered in, wanting to see the "doctor."

The guards claimed maladies of all sorts, with symptoms ranging from headaches to insomnia to sore throats and lung infections. The first one in line had a bad cough. Larry took it upon himself to diagnose the problem. While I rummaged through the kit, Larry, wearing a sympathetic frown, told the fellow to quit smoking. He made an X with his fingers and pointed to the pack of cigarettes in the guard's shirt pocket. That got some laughs, and a few jeers, because *everyone*—even Bedouin children—smokes potent, tar-laden Arab cigarettes. It bought me some time, however, to fish out a bottle labeled "Sleeping Pills. Caution . . . will cause drowsiness."

Sleeping pills? It gave me an idea. I showed them to Larry, who raised an eyebrow, then nodded as if to say, "What can we lose? Go for it!" I addressed the smoker. "Drink plenty of water," I said, "and take a few of these." I handed him three sleeping pills, which he eagerly swallowed. Then he stepped aside.

Soon I was doling out the pills to the entire garrison. I handed each guard three or four capsules along with my confident prognosis—"This will help your headache," "This will soothe your stomach"—until practically the entire corps had ingested a potent dose of sedatives. When the last of the townsfolk left and the guards returned to their posts, Larry and I sat down against the wall and waited.

Within twenty minutes, the pills started to kick in. First some of the Bedouins started to fidget, then nod. Some began to yawn, while others searched for a cozy spot to nap. The commander tossed a camel saddle on the dirt floor for a pillow and covered it with a blanket; two others tilted back, glassy eyed, against the concrete wall. We held our breaths, scarcely believing what we were seeing. It was like an episode of the old *Mutual of Omaha's Wild Kingdom* series, where Marlin Perkins shoots the bear with a tranquilizer dart, then watches it teeter and stumble and topple into the net. The guards moved like drugged bears, swaying back and forth, tipping off balance, then falling sound asleep. In less than forty-five minutes, the whole cell block was drooling, mumbling, and snoring like chainsaws.

With a single exception.

One surly young guard had refused to take our pills. He was about nineteen years old and all business, though nothing in his training prepared him for such a bizarre turn of events. We watched as he began murmuring to himself, pacing nervously, trying to shake his comrades awake. No one moved, which heightened his alarm. He started waving his pistol threateningly in our direction.

Pistol or not, Larry and I realized this was probably our only chance to escape. We knew if we waited around until everyone woke up, our ruse would be exposed. We'd never get out alive. So, with the guard agitated and distracted by his friends, we

144

quietly put on our shoes and socks. Then, smiling and nodding deferentially, we started walking very slowly from the cell block toward the truck. The guard stopped what he was doing and followed us, waving his pistol in our direction. We stayed calm, bowing politely. Yet we noticed in his manner a youthful indecision, an apparent reluctance to use the gun. With his sidekicks snoring in the dust, he seemed to have lost his nerve.

We kept walking toward the truck, holding our breaths. I slowly opened the door, turned the key, and gave it some gas. Waving warmly to the curious villagers now gathered about, we were about to drive off . . . when the young Bedouin flew into a rage. He screamed at the top of his lungs and ran in front of our truck. He pointed the pistol at Larry's head—I fully expected him to shoot us both. But just as suddenly, he motioned with his pistol for us to stay put. He called for one of the younger boys, and together they hopped in a green, military-looking pickup parked next to ours. With a wave of his arm and a loud shout, the Frontier guard ordered us to follow him. He popped the clutch and sped away, into the wilderness. The next few moments found us careening like maniacs away from the outpost, across the desert floor, following our livid young jailer to God knows where.

Sixteen

CRISIS IN TABUK

> O God, you are my God,
> earnestly I seek you;
> my soul thirsts for you,
> my body longs for you,
> in a dry and weary land
> where there is no water (Ps. 63:1).

As we bounced along the washboard floor of the desert at sixty miles per hour, Larry decided to climb into the back of the pickup to dispose of the implicating evidence we had stashed there: infrared scopes, maps, film, and metal detection equipment. He dangled out the side of the truck, clinging to the open door, like in those old cowboy movies where the hero leaps from the stagecoach to the team of stampeding horses. Ahead about fifty yards sped the Bedouin guard and his young assistant, driving like maniacs. Lucky for us their truck kicked up such a huge cloud of dust that we gained a temporary smoke screen, camouflaging our efforts.

We had decided they probably were hustling us off to a larger jail for a full-scale interrogation. All they knew was that their post commander and all the other guards had fallen asleep. So they were probably taking us to Tabuk, where they would hand us over to professional police who would no doubt decide our fate through a tough grilling and a bolt-by-bolt search of our pickup.

We couldn't understand why these Frontier Police hadn't separated us, but it allowed us time to get our story straight and plan our strategy—which included ridding ourselves of all the evidence in our pickup. And do it *before* we hit paved highway, while the dust cloud still gave us some cover. We had endured one close call already. Just minutes after leaving the frontier outpost, I tried to slow down and let the Bedouin race ahead so we could start discarding contraband without being seen in his rearview mirror. But the instant I reduced speed, the Bedouin slammed on his brakes, leapt from his truck, ran back, and pointed his gun at my head. Then, with wild shouts and threatening gestures, he rapped the pistol's muzzle on the speedometer as if to say—"Hurry up! Hurry up!" The message was clear: keep up or else.

We barreled overland, without a path or trail, reaching suicidal speeds as we rammed into fat dunes, clattered across rock-strewn gullies, and bottomed out over brush-covered ridges. The truck, along with our necks and tailbones, was taking a pounding, and I fought just to keep it upright. The jagged terrain finally leveled out into a vast, rose-colored valley, whose gentle hillocks and soft floor glowed crimson in the mid-afternoon glare.

Judging from our compass, we knew for certain the Bedouin was headed to Tabuk. And for an irrational few moments, we considered making a break for it. "I could cut north and speed toward the Jordanian border, try to lose the Bedouin, and pray we don't get lost," I proposed. But that was a best-case scenario; the Jordanian border lay 150 miles away, and we didn't know the terrain. Even if we made it, we probably would be denied access. And even if we did give him the slip, we'd be fugitives from justice, subjects of a full-scale manhunt—and an escape attempt, added to the trespassing and spying charges we likely faced, would assure our swift execution. But the most likely scenario was that the Bedouin would chase us down inside of a mile and shoot us on the spot.

We nixed the escape plan.

But still we had to lose the evidence. "We've *got* to get rid of this stuff," Larry said. "Try lagging back again, only this time do it very *slowly. Gradually.*"

It was do or die. Over the next ten miles, I began to reduce my speed, slowly . . . cautiously . . . imperceptibly . . . until the interval between our trucks, still choked by clouds of dust, was sufficient to obscure the Bedouin's view. "Go!" I shouted. "Hop out—quick! We don't have much time."

Clawing and grappling his way out the door, Larry did his best stunt-man impersonation. He climbed up and over the rear fender, collapsing into the pickup bed. He wasted no time tossing everything overboard: our infrared binoculars, the metal detector, batteries and battery chargers, all of our topographical and satellite maps, shovels, ropes, gloves—finally, even the cans of gas and boxes of water. By the time he finished, the desert floor, littered with expensive outfitters gear, looked like a ransacked army surplus store. When Larry started in on the rock samples, however, jettisoning the precious chips and shards we'd gathered, it felt like parting with our own children. We had risked our lives to get those samples, and now, simply to throw them away . . . well, we couldn't do it. They were just too important to our mission. We kept a cache of smaller stones under the tarp in hopes they'd be overlooked as common rubble.

The pickup bed virtually emptied, I leaned over and opened the door. In perfect form, Larry grabbed it and swung his legs and torso back inside the cab, absorbing several punishing body shots from the lurching chassis. "OK, now, good," I said, "but you have another job to do. Take the grill off the air vent on the dashboard. I think we can hide one roll of film." My police training had taught me a technique drug smugglers use to hide contraband. Larry used his Swiss Army knife to remove the grill, then placed a single roll of film inside—the one with our shots of the altar and pillars. "OK," I said, "now stuff one of your black socks over the opening and replace the grill. The black cloth makes the vent appear empty and hopefully won't attract anyone's attention." Larry threw the rest of the film out the window.

It still bothers me that some of our best photos lie buried beneath a dune somewhere in the Saudi desert. In hindsight, we probably didn't have to toss everything, but we believed we would be searched from head to toe, our car ransacked. So out went everything but the clothes on our backs, a couple of rocks, a roll of film, and our cameras. By the time we hit paved highway, we were squeaky clean.

THE INTERROGATION

Arriving in Tabuk after a two-hour scramble, our hearts sank as the Bedouin pulled up to a T-intersection at the gate of a massive, cement-block prison. *Would we be taken directly there?* Its forty-foot-high walls, guard towers, and rows of barbed wire conjured harrowing images of the movie *Midnight Express*. "If he drives in there," said Larry, disconsolate, "it's all over." We sat at the light, truck idling, mulling another escape attempt— this time a mad dash into the chaos of the city. But when the stoplight changed, the Bedouin turned left, away from the prison. We followed him to a small police station at the center of town.

Neither of us was physically or psychologically prepared for a rigorous inquisition. It had been a savage, pressure-filled road race through the Saudi outback, in temperatures ranging between 110 and 115 degrees. We had spent the previous night dodging Bedouin sentries on Jabal al Lawz and had neither food nor drink (except bitter tea) since our arrest. It had been even longer since we slept. We were running on sheer adrenaline as the Bedouin led us into the station.

The Frontier cop brought us to another holding tank, similar to the desert cell but with clean carpeting, a few Arabic pillows propped against a wall, and a wobbly ceiling fan that provided a thin draft in the stifling heat. And then . . . *nothing*. No interrogation, no arrest. Just more waiting. No one seemed to know what to say or how to approach us.

Which wasn't necessarily good news. The longer we languished in jail, the worse our prospects of getting out of the kingdom. We had to resolve the situation soon. The Bedouin cop seemed determined to detain us; our cameras and passports already had been confiscated, and the Tabuk police acted surly, convinced we were guilty of *something*—spying, trespassing, they didn't know. Any minute now someone's superior would show up and settle the matter . . . a frightening thought.

At first Larry and I acted unfailingly polite, nonconfrontational, cooperative to a fault. We kept smiling and joking, trying to establish a rapport and explain ourselves to whoever would listen. Larry did magic tricks for some of the cops and young jailhouse assistants, lads also charged with this station's abominable tea-serving rites.

When they finally let us alone, I whispered, "Larry, we can't wait for something to happen. We have to *make* something happen, *now*, or we're going to end up in prison." Though neither of us knew exactly what that meant, we decided it was time to stand our ground and demand our rights as American citizens. We knew it was a risky move, but we couldn't stomach the thought of another hour within these menacing walls.

We didn't have to wait long. I had already produced our truck rental agreement, hoping to prove we were merely tourists, not spies. Instead, they ordered us to turn over the papers, which Larry refused. He ripped the papers off the counter and unleashed a diatribe that—even if they couldn't understand a word he said—told them we were through being pushed around.

"We've been held up here for eight hours now!" he screamed, pounding his fist on the counter. "We're *sick* and *tired* of the way we've been treated. We've done nothing wrong. The cameral you have contains pictures of scrub brush and camels. And if you don't believe us, you can develop the film and see for yourselves." He told them we didn't know we were on a military reservation and certainly weren't aware that cameras were banned. He protested bitterly about being forced at gunpoint to drive through the desert at such high speeds, arguing that we probably ruined the truck and "will be forced to pay a severe damage penalty." Finally, as a *coup de grace*, Larry threw up his arms and bellowed, "We're tired. We're hungry. We haven't eaten for thirteen hours. We're being treated like criminals, and . . ." he turned and looked square into the Bedouin's eyes, "we're *sick* of your blasted tea!"

153
Λ

Seventeen

DELIVERANCE

What an inspired performance! The guards' mouths hung open. Larry's tirade seemed to soften their resolve, and they let us hang on to the truck rental agreement. But as we got up to leave, they ordered us at gunpoint to sit back down. They weren't releasing us.

It was time for Plan B. We had agreed our next step would be to get permission to use a phone, hoping to call the Tabuk Sahara, our hotel on the last trip. I reminded Larry that the Egyptian hotel manager had been quite friendly to us, seemed none too fond of the Saudis, and, more importantly, spoke fluent English. If we could connect with him somehow, he might agree to intercede, or at least translate, on our behalf—perhaps tell the police our side of the story. Maybe he could help us get these stalled negotiations out of neutral. The police, appearing impatient with this game of cat and mouse, consented to let us use their phone.

Thumbing through the Yellow Pages (yes, even the Saudis have Yellow Pages), we couldn't tell one listing from another, since everything was, naturally, in Arabic. Larry pulled out our truck rental agreement and dialed the number on the paper. An English-speaking manager answered and cheerfully provided us the hotel's phone number. Within minutes we had the manager of the Tabuk Sahara on the line. When we explained our predicament, we were amazed at how eager he was to plead our case. He asked to speak with the Bedouin cop, and told him firmly we were just tourists, that we wanted our cameras and passports back, and that we demanded our freedom. Next, he arranged for the police to take us to the hotel—"neutral turf," he said—where chances of negotiating our release would be more favorable. The Bedouin cop clearly opposed the idea, yet at the urging of the Tabuk officers, he finally relented and drove us to the hotel, accompanied by a contingent of armed police. Larry summed up our dilemma: "Who needs an American consulate when you've got an Egyptian hotel director?"

At the hotel, the manager—a short, slender, bearded fellow with a jolly disposition—met us in the lobby. With a look of concern he pulled us aside and whispered: "Gentlemen, I think I can be of help. Please follow my lead. I am going to take you into my office and scold you very harshly. Don't take it personally. I am just doing this for show for the Bedouin—he is a very hard case. He wants you to stand trial." How deeply humbling, that this man who knew nothing about us—except that we'd stayed at the hotel once, paid our bill, and were pleasant to his staff—would rise to our defense. "A little common courtesy goes a long way over here," I told Larry as we entered the manager's office.

There he commenced to yell and swear at us, ranting and raving and scolding, ordering us never to bring cameras into the kingdom again. If we did, he said, the Bedouins would handcuff us and throw us into jail for the rest of our lives. When he finished, he winked at us and said, "Now pretend you are very sorry and sincere about all this."

Larry and I bowed repeatedly and said we felt awful about the terrible misunderstanding. For a moment the Bedouin's icy resolve seemed to melt. He appeared about to let us leave—but then his jaw clenched and his countenance hardened. I think he suspected us of drugging his compatriots and decided to stand firm. Another stalemate.

The tension grew so thick you could practically see it—the Bedouin was *not* going to let us go. I thought it was going to end badly for us when Larry suddenly turned rude and surly. We had tried to show we were men of good will and intent, but Larry had reached his boiling point. He began arguing, then yelling at the officer, telling him he had no right to hold us, and to "free us this instant." Soon they were yelling back and forth in dialects neither could understand. The hotel manager looked mortified, and I just stood there watching, rivulets of sweat running down my back.

Without warning, Larry decided to go for broke. He pulled our forged letter of sponsorship from his back pocket, and, like Errol Flynn, slammed it on the table. "We're guests of the *king!*" Larry shouted. "And if you don't let us go, you'll have to answer to *him.*" I felt my stomach sink to the floor. Larry had played our trump card, and now the blade of the guillotine hung directly over our heads. Larry hadn't even told me he'd *brought* the old letter, which purported to show that the king himself had invited us into the country. All I could do was look into the Bedouin's steely eyes, trying not to blink.

Larry told the hotel manager to read the letter to the police, who stood scratching their heads. We could see they were questioning themselves, wondering if they had indeed arrested two men the king himself had invited into the country. In the ultimate game of high-stakes poker, Larry risked everything on a calculated guess they wouldn't try to contact the Saudi king. They stared at us. We stared back. I knew the Saudi king is revered as Allah's right hand, a man you don't want to upset— a prospect which seemed to set the guards back on their heels. By now they were jabbering back and forth in a far corner of the room. When, after a long moment of silence, the Bedouin returned from his mini-conference, it was clear the tone of negotiations had shifted in our favor. They blinked first.

With a suddenness that startled even the hotel manager, the Bedouin, still livid, threw up his hands and slammed our cameras and passports on the table. "I believe you are free to go," said the hotel manager.

We were free!

Larry and I stared at one another in disbelief as the Bedouin marched toward the door with his armed retinue in tow. He spun to face us once more, his eyes flashing rage. With one last, violent shake of his finger, he warned us that if we *ever* came back into his area, we would be thrown in jail. He spit out a word—*kalibush!*—then crossed his wrists in front, like they were handcuffed. Then he spewed more ugly threats about cameras and spying and prison. Larry and I became the picture of repentance, nodding humbly and bowing with downcast eyes, making many apologies. The Bedouin at last turned and stormed out of the hotel. And with that staggering turn, our incarceration ended.

Larry's bottom lip quivered. Errol Flynn had bet the farm on a worthless deed and won. *No wonder he is such a good businessman*, I thought. *Nerves of steel.*

It should have been time to rejoice, but in our exhausted state it took every fiber of will to avoid dropping to our knees and sobbing. We turned to the hotel manager and showered him with thanks. He smiled warmly, pleased to have been of assistance. But then he bowed curtly and, without a trace of sentiment, said, "I would suggest you make arrangements to leave the country as soon as possible. That officer might return. He was not fully convinced by your story."

Our Egyptian host graciously accommodated us with a hotel room, where we showered, ordered pitchers of orange juice, and ate a quick room-service meal. Then we cleaned out the truck and drove quickly to a downtown travel office, where Larry threw his Gold Card on the table and said, "I don't care how much it costs. Get us on the first flight to the United States." We had arrived at the hotel under armed guard at 5 P.M.— sweaty, dirty, hungry—and so tired we could barely stand. By 8:55 P.M. we had flown out of Tabuk and were checked through the Jedda airport en route to Riyadh.

HOMEWARD BOUND

At Riyadh's spotless, cosmopolitan international airport, Larry was able to purchase, at great expense, two nonstop tickets to

New York City's JFK Airport. But before being allowed into the terminal, we had to pass through seven checkpoints where our luggage and passports were rigorously inspected. We breezed through without incident, a testimony to our meticulous evidence-disposal job in the desert. We walked to the departure gate, where we endured an agonizing, two-hour delay before takeoff.

Every minute seemed like an eternity. *Had the Bedouin changed his mind or checked out our story? Had he found some of our film or the metal detector on his drive back to the desert? Had he ordered a kingdomwide warrant for our arrest?* Our imaginations, magnified by fatigue, ran wild. Every soldier that walked by with a gun—and, trust me, soldiers with guns are *everywhere* in the kingdom—incited cold sweats and made my heart pound like a piston. Larry and I were both flexed tight as drums, certain the Bedouin was coming for us, until the moment the plane arrived.

But the departure door opened. We took our seats. The plane doors closed. *Ahhh . . . Sweet Jesus!* We were finally headed home.

Once we buckled in, sleep beckoned. Three days without shut-eye, under the most stressful conditions, hit us both with sledgehammer force. I stayed awake long enough to convince the man sitting between Larry and me to sit somewhere else. Then I collapsed across three seats. Larry inflated his high-tech air mattress and slunk to the floor, sprawled between seat supports. We both fell dead asleep before the plane lifted off. We remained motionless for the entire thirteen-hour trip to New York, where we awoke in the same position.

After deplaning, we didn't talk much. Larry had to catch a connecting flight at another terminal and my flight home to Colorado Springs wouldn't leave for a couple of hours. We hugged and said good-bye. As he walked away, he looked over his shoulder and with a weary, hangdog smile, said, "Talk to you later. I'm going home to be with my family."

I wandered aimlessly about the concourse, watching people, trying to let the reality of the past three days sink in. What did it mean to actually be *home* after such an ordeal? I'd shared an incredible adventure, been involved, perhaps, in one of the greatest archaeological discoveries of all time. Yet it felt unreal, as if it had happened in a dream—or to someone else. It surely wasn't me dangling off that cliff at three in the morning, or touching those altars and pillars. Surely not me!

Lost in thought, I boarded the plane for my last leg home. High in the sky, watching the clouds float below me, and beneath them the green-brown lattice of mid-America, I breathed out an ardent, "Thank you, Lord. *I made it!*" That much was real— he *had* delivered me. He shouldn't have, but he did. I knew because *it* was still there, the peace that blanketed my soul during those wrenching moments when death seemed certain. Now, against all odds, I was on my way home. Soon I would be with my family, hugging my children, my wife. In that moment I believed I was the most blessed, unworthy man on earth, privileged as none other. *I* had stood on Mount Sinai! And by all accounts, I would live to tell about it.

Ah yes—to *tell* about it. That promised to be another adventure in itself. But I'd think about that later.

I leaned my head back, closed my eyes, and broke into an enormous grin. Then, with my head turned toward the window, I said in a whisper so soft and quiet it seemed to emanate from somewhere or someone else—"God, I made you a promise. I'm all yours."

And with a certainty that has never waned, I knew I was.

Part Two

THE SEARCH FOR PHARAOH'S CHARIOTS

Eighteen

THE BIBLE SAYS IT'S SO!

How is it that one of history's most distinctive mountains got lost? Or was it merely misplaced? And what of the mountain most think is Mount Sinai, in Egypt? One thing's clear: since the fourth century A.D.—when Emperor Constantine's mother, Queen Helena, said she saw it in a vision—the peak at St. Catherine's Monastery has made the loudest (if not well-founded) claims to being the real deal. It now anchors the region's tourism industry and remains the principal reason why, if you ask anyone on a tour bus in Cairo or strolling the streets of Tel Aviv, "Where is Mount Sinai?" they'll say without blinking, "At St. Catherine's Monastery!" It's practically a reflex, like saying Mount Rushmore is in South Dakota.

This cadre of believers includes many modern scholars and historians who provide the data needed to make the maps of the holy lands found in most Bibles. Turn in any Bible to the schematics of ancient Palestine and the Sinai

Peninsula, and you'll likely see small, triangle-shaped graphics scattered about denoting important Exodus landmarks, like the springs at Marah and Elim, or the Hebrew campsites at Dophkah and Rephidim. Look at the southern tip of the Sinai Peninsula. There you'll notice Mount Sinai, also called Jebel Musa, or Mountain of Moses.

A closer look at most editions, however, reveals something odd that should stop even a beginning Bible student in his tracks: small, subtle question marks (?) nuzzled in beside these landmarks. Why question marks? Why call into question the whereabouts of landmarks that tradition tells us we should take for granted?

As amazing as it sounds, the precise location of these monuments remains a mystery. Most maps highlighting Exodus-route markers are no better than a geographic version of pin-the-tail-on-the-donkey. Biblical landmarks that might reveal, say, the specific route used by the Israelites to flee Pharaoh or the true crossing point on the Red Sea—both of which would point one unequivocally to the real Mount Sinai—remain ever-shifting targets, objects of persistent debate.

Take, for instance, a fascinating fact of which the average tourist to Egypt isn't aware: the peak at St. Catherine's is but one of several (at last count, *twelve*) mountains to be named, at various times, the *real* Mount Sinai. Most can still be found in the Sinai Peninsula, located anywhere from Serbal and Safsafa in the south, to Serabit el-Khadem and Sin Bishar in the central peninsula, and as far north as Halal and Karkom. Some scholars place it in the Negev highlands, while others swear it's not in Egypt at all but somewhere in Arabia.

166

All those unknowns illustrate the cardinal tenet of any search for Mount Sinai: to find the mountain, you first have to know, *Which way did the Israelites go?* It's the pivotal question of Exodus apologetics, the connecting link of any successful attempt to pinpoint the mountain. Locating Mount Sinai requires a rigorous deciphering of which way, how far—even how fast—the Israelites traveled in their flight from Pharaoh to the sea. The Mount Sinai surplus has more to do with the glut of possible Exodus routes than with any particular mountain's bearing or appearance. And since these theories can't all be right, we find ourselves back at square one—where *is* it?

A STUNNING REPORT

When I stumbled into this chaotic state of affairs in 1988, on the eve of my first trip to Egypt, Dick Ewing and Roy Knuteson, patrons of the mission to find Pharaoh's chariots, had been wrestling with the riddle for more than a decade. Having hoped for a simple, concise review of the facts (thinking it would move them swiftly toward their goal), they were shocked to find virtually no consensus among the vast volumes written on Israel's forty-year sojourn in the desert. Seemingly innocuous details of the march's timing, origin, duration, and direction— any of which would bring the hunt into sharp focus—blurred and vanished in an archaeological potluck of dangling theories and gross contradictions. Knuteson began to question the underlying techniques of modern research. Had any of these experts ever *visited* the region to see for themselves?

Knuteson's wry appraisal, after a thorough review: "Many of the writers in this area of information were novices, having neither visited the area first-hand, nor researching it well, since most seemed to be simply quoting a few older authors. Most had no regard to the facts of the Exodus, and most of the material was old and outdated."

This unsettling dilemma frustrated their search. Solace came only in a growing suspicion that most everyone had been looking for the stations of the Exodus in the wrong places. They spent the next few years piecing together a version of events that repudiated widely held notions, such as the traditional view that the entire forty-year Exodus wanderings took place within the Sinai Peninsula.

To suggest that the Exodus ventured *outside* the landlocked, forty thousand square miles of the Sinai cut hard against the grain of mainstream thought and certainly would have sparked a hail of criticism—were it not for the 1984 release of a breakthrough report out of Egypt, published in *Biblical Archaeology Review*. The article profiled the research of a prominent team of Israeli archaeologists who had just completed a fifteen-year exploration in Egypt's Sinai Peninsula. These professionals excavated with a fine-tooth comb nearly every site ever thought to be associated with the Exodus, and their findings revealed nothing! Fifteen years of exhaustive, painstaking investigation by veteran archaeologists found nothing to suggest as many as two-and-a-half million Jewish pilgrims once flooded the Egyptian landscape. No traces of a mighty host littering the wilderness with their smoking campfires, stores of food, cook pots, and acres of pottery, ceremonial implements and utensils, weapons, jewels, trinkets, and religious objects. No evidence of huge herds, flocks, or the daily waste and abandoned junk of a wandering multitude. Nothing.

The scientists found not so much as a hint that a throng of humanity had visited the countryside for even a day, much less for forty years. Their report in *Biblical Archaeology Review* stated, "Although there are dozens of theories (of the Exodus occurring in the Sinai Peninsula), none is supported by archaeological evidence. And much as we had hoped otherwise, our recent explorations have not advanced us toward a solution. Nowhere in Sinai did we or our colleagues find any concrete remains of the stations on the Exodus route, nor even small encampments that could be attributed to the relevant period. Neither did we discover anything that would help us identify the Mount of God. So the enigma—and the challenge—remain." [1]

How, Knuteson and Ewing wondered, had a team of experienced archaeologists, using the best equipment and technology available, failed to find what nearly every page of Exodus literature said *must* have been there? What did it mean?

For Ewing and Knuteson, it meant vindication. It meant they could now unyoke themselves from generations of handed-down wisdom and set their sights elsewhere. It meant they were free to ponder what the Bible might have to say on the subject.

GOD'S MAP

In 1988 these dogged explorers were ready to set off for Egypt to search for the chariot wheels of Pharaoh's drowned army. I arrived with the others at Ewing's home in Portland the week before our departure, to rehearse our game plan and plot our undersea exploration. Everything had been laid out in meticulous detail, each stage mapped, charted, and scheduled. Ewing told me how the mission's success rested on a steely faith in the absolute accuracy of the Bible, and that, almost to a man, the team believed the Bible to be the inspired Word of God—was, in fact, (according to 2 Tim. 3:16) "God-breathed." He emphasized that this inspired document included all historic, geographic, and numeric details of the great Exodus.

"On *this* trip, Bob," he said, "the Bible is to be interpreted literally. It will be our primary map, our primary resource in our hunt for Pharaoh's chariots. All other information, regardless of the author, will be tested against that which is already revealed in Scripture."

I stood there, speechless. They had discarded their textbooks and settled on the Bible as their sole guide. Modern books, maps—the simple, time-tested tools of modern inquiry I'd come to trust as a crime scene investigator—were to be left behind! I had joined a team of grown men convinced the Bible *alone* was trustworthy. It was to them a genuinely divine resource, free of man's flawed interpretations. And they were sure it would lead us straight to our prize! I recall thinking, *I'm glad I don't have money invested in this enterprise.*

WHERE IS MOUNT SINAI?

But as I was soon to discover, the Bible held clues and answers to questions most scholars hadn't thought to ask. And the Bible is where our quest begins: with a simple, brutally clear verse of Scripture. Galatians 4:25 states, "Now Hagar stands for Mount Sinai in Arabia." It's one of several Bible references plainly describing the location of Mount Sinai. It's in *Arabia*. Not in Egypt. Not in the Sinai Peninsula.

And how does the Bible define *Arabia?* In both the Old and New Testaments, Arabia has always been located south and *east* of Palestine, the area of present-day Saudi Arabia. The Sinai Peninsula, on the other hand, lies south and *west* of Palestine. The apostle Paul, under the inspiration of the Holy Spirit, informs us that Mount Sinai is in Saudi Arabia. Not Egypt!

On the strength of this verse alone, we could make a case against the idea of Mount Sinai lying anywhere in the Sinai Peninsula. We could in good conscience denounce the peak at St. Catherine's as a fraud and unravel centuries of speculation. We might well argue that, were the Bible given its due as a historical resource, we wouldn't need archaeologists to tell us where the Mountain of God is. A short verse in Galatians should answer the question for all time.

But if Scripture makes it so clear Mount Sinai is *not* in Egypt, why does every map in every Bible in every Christian bookstore tell me that's where it is? Why do thousands of tourists (and even, recently, the pope himself) flock each year to St. Catherine's Monastery to genuflect at the foot of an Egyptian impostor? Why all the confusion?

It's largely because, from ancient times to the present, too few have regarded the Bible as a reliable guide to these ancient sites. Couple this with the fact that relatively few modern historians have visited the lands where these events occurred, and we gain insight into the mystery.

In our adventure to find Pharaoh's chariot wheels, the Bible unfolded for us like a *Rand McNally Road Atlas*. The Word of God served as our infallible compass, pointing us to a stagger-

171

ing succession of venerated localities "lost" by modernity. In the Book of Exodus we discovered how far, and how fast, the Israelites fled from Egypt to the Red Sea; from Isaiah we learned of a road in the middle of the deep. So with Bibles in hand, we headed to Egypt and to the land where it all began: Goshen.

Nineteen

CHARMED IN GOSHEN

> Pharaoh said to Joseph, "Your father and
> your brothers have come to you, and the
> land of Egypt is before you; settle your
> father and your brothers in the best part
> of the land. Let them live in Goshen"
> (Gen. 47:5–6).

For a westerner like myself, Goshen can overload the senses. A kaleidoscope of colors, sounds, and smells parallels those found in other subtropical climates, but here an endless, blistering desert bounds the land on all sides. It's a bit unnerving. As is the culture.

I saw the rifle before I saw the child. From the shadows of a roadside shanty, the young boy strayed into our path. He held a rifle to his chin and swung it in our direction. Thinking *"Terrorist!"* we ducked behind our seats. Our Egyptian bus driver slammed on the brakes (he was either trying to avoid hitting the child or stopping to surrender—I couldn't tell). The boy smiled. He calmly turned and fired a single shot into the air. I peered over the seat in time to see a bird drop from the sky at his feet, a pigeon. The child giggled as he knelt down to look at his limp prize; he carried it back to the covered stoop of the mud shanty, where a woman stood holding a butcher knife. I was flabbergasted. Without aiming, the kid knocked a bird out of the sky with one shot, like the elite marksmen I'd known on the SWAT force.

With our mouths hanging open, our eyes drifted skyward. Along the village roof line stretched an intricate network of mud towers, looking for all the world like a line of giant chocolate ice cream cones. Each cone contained dozens of little holes in which hundreds of roosting pigeons cooed, preened, and fussed—a pigeon feedlot of sorts, maintained by locals as a quick-stop meat counter. Each afternoon at dusk moms sent their sons outside with long rifles to bag dinner.

The incident captured for me the lively pace and easy abundance of this fabled land, the launch site of the great Exodus. This was my first taste of Goshen—balmy, moist, and outlandishly animated. Here, in Egypt's Upper Nile Delta, we would begin our ill-fated search for Pharaoh's chariots. The cameras rolled as Dick Ewing and Roy Knuteson collected footage of Goshen for their documentary.

Aside from the motorized chaos of the roadways, it seemed little had changed here in the thirty-five hundred years since Pharaoh gave Goshen as a gift to the descendants of Jacob. It served as the world's breadbasket during a great famine and remains a stunningly beautiful land, sandwiched by miles of lush vegetation. No wonder Pharaoh called it the "best part of the land" in all of Egypt!

My eyes fastened upon the rainbow splash of pastel pinks, yellows, luminescent blues, and purples dancing off this lush, irrigated oasis. Our bus sped along ancient dirt lanes humming with bicycle taxis and backfiring scooters zipping in and out of wobbly buffalo carts. Wagons creaked under bushels of leeks, onions, and dates. Everywhere we saw barefoot kids in shorts and Tom Cruise T-shirts jostling by the side of the road, moving to the same comic rhythm as the scruffy chickens pecking and scratching at the edge of our wheels. We passed a man with a face as wide and glowering as a camel saddle, hawking candy by loudspeaker from his crimson pushcart. Despite his frightening looks, flocks of children swarmed about him. He must have sold a good product.

Best part of the land, indeed. No wonder a paltry seventy Israelites (Gen. 46:26)—direct descendants of Jacob accompanying their patriarch to Goshen—could in a few short years multiply and prosper until they became "exceedingly numerous," until the land was "filled with them" (Exod. 1:7). Such a fearsome population explosion ignited a furious backlash among the Egyptians. Fearing the Hebrews would overrun the country with their flocks and property, Pharaoh pressed them into brutal, forced labor, leading ultimately to a decree that every newborn Hebrew male was to be killed.

Our bus cruised past the bustling bazaars of the Nile. I pictured Moses born into a world both beautiful and mysterious, left in a basket among the reeds of the Nile, adopted by Pharaoh's daughter, and reared as a child of royalty in Pharaoh's court. Who knew then he would become the hero of Exodus?

Goshen, of course, became a central player in the unfolding drama. Moses fled Goshen after killing an Egyptian oppressor. Forty years later he returned, touched by God, to lead his people to freedom. Pharaoh proved a stubborn nemesis, but Goshen presented the bigger problem. The Israelites didn't want to leave this land of splendor, preferring to be slaves in paradise than free and ill at ease. They pined for Goshen's succulent food and tangy spices. They longed for its lavish excess. "If only we had died by the LORD's hand in Egypt!" they complained. "There we sat around pots of meat and ate all the food we wanted, but you have brought us out into this desert to starve this entire assembly to death" (Exod. 16:3).

Even in bondage they had grown complacent. It's easy to see why. Goshen's canals snake through miles of plush farmland in stunning patchwork; its rich, molasses earth boasts sleek, lazy rivers which fan out like a giant palm toward the Mediterranean. Vast, billowing fields of cotton, maize, and rice garnish the verdant landscape, and everywhere water buffalos graze, plow, and turn wheels for grinding grain. Fleshy palms and iridescent green fields fill the horizon with row upon row of crops linked by soft, trickling streams festooned with rustic paddle wheels. Traveling from Goshen into the adjacent desert, unimaginably hot and forsaken, I understood something else: God *had* to put the Israelites into bondage, or he might never have been able to pry them away. They might be there still.

THE BITTER LAKES

From emerald valleys we crossed under the Gulf of Suez—lined with huge cargo ships, tankers, and military frigates—into the bleak, dead desert. It was the Bitter Lakes region. While the

Delta is lush and beautiful, the Bitter Lakes are a brutally hot, mosquito-infested wasteland of marshy bogs and shallow, muddy lakes. It blew our minds to think that many modern scholars believe these squalid pools (also known as the Sea of Reeds) to be the "deep waters" of the Red Sea cited in Scripture.

It was like passing from Hawaii to Death Valley, like stepping from paradise into hell. In a heartbeat, leafy delta vanishes into stinging badlands. Remnants of the bloody Six Days War— Egypt's short, bloody confrontation with Israel in June 1967—were everywhere. Our bus climbed a sandy ridge to behold the charred husks of two armored tanks, one Israeli, one Egyptian. Their facing positions told of a surprise encounter, of meeting at the ridge and firing off simultaneous rounds. Only shrapnel remained of the left side of the Egyptian tank; the Israeli cannon turret looked like an exploded cigar. Barbed wire, foxhole trenches, rotting sandbags, sandblasted war bunkers, and the rusted pieces of antiaircraft guns and mobile artillery littered the desert.

Bitter Lakes indeed! And Knuteson knew all about them. The Bitter Lakes are also known as the Sea of Reeds, a place where three generations of scholars suspect the Israelites crossed the Red Sea. They argue the Bitter Lakes is what the Bible really means when it says "Red Sea," a theory made possible by the handy access of these lakes to Goshen and the unwieldy Hebrew term *Red Sea*.

On a map the lakes appear huge, like a bonafide inland sea. In person they're little more than a marshy system of mud flats, flea-infested bogs, and shallow, algae-covered wetlands. And

177

while it wouldn't take much more than a good stiff wind to blow them apart (a theory popular with many supporters), a close-up look reveals the lunacy of associating them with the Red Sea of biblical acclaim.

First, the Red Sea is one of the deepest bodies of water on earth, so in any discussion about it, depth must be a major factor. In Exodus the Red Sea is described as an immense tidal basin whose "*deep* waters" formed a "wall of water on their right and on their left," and whose waters engulfed and drowned an entire Egyptian army. Scripture speaks with one voice about the Red Sea:

> "The deep waters have covered them;
>   they sank to the depths like a stone" (Exod. 15:5).

> "He rebuked the Red Sea, and it dried up;
>   he led them through the depths as through a
>   desert" (Ps. 106:9).

> "The sea engulfed their enemies" (emphasis added,
>   Ps. 78:53).

Taking the Bible at face value, we must accept that the children of Israel walked through a veritable Niagra Falls of suspended water.

Turn from that mighty sea to the Bitter Lakes—a mud puddle by comparison. They are anything but deep and never have been much deeper than they are now. Far from presenting Pharaoh with a real threat of drowning, the biggest obstacle these lakes could threaten was muddy sandals.

If these shallow lakes are the real Red Sea crossing point, then the Mountain of God must lie somewhere nearby—say, at St. Catherine's Monastery, or at any of the dozens of sites cluttering the Sinai Peninsula. Here we come to an intellectual moment of truth that must be faced.

RED VERSUS REED SEA

A scholarly paper written in the mid-1800s made some spurious observations about the Bitter Lakes, claiming they were the actual Red Sea of the Exodus.[1] As so often happens in the name of research, that thesis, published in a prominent journal of the day, formed the backbone of a long succession of articles and papers. After decades of dutiful replication, a full-blown scholarly tradition emerged. To this day, that thesis and its conclusions are quoted and footnoted by historians and theologians as if it were gospel.

179
Λ

But if the original premise is flawed, so must be its conclusions—and future generations end up with a distorted view of history. To have any hope of separating truth from opinion, we must take a fresh look at the facts. In this case, we must work backward to trace the meaning of the original Hebrew words for Red Sea (*Yam Suph*). Herein lies the heart of the controversy.

First, no one disputes the meaning of the Hebrew word *yam*, which simply means "sea." The problem lies in the translation of the word *Suph* (or *sup*). Some say it means "red," as in Red Sea; others say it means "reed," as in Reed Sea. The debate rages over the etymology of *Suph*.

So which is it? Does *Yam Suph* mean Red Sea or Reed Sea? The Hebrew seems to leave the door open to both. Most recent translations of the Bible—including the Revised Standard Version, the New American Standard Bible, the New English Bible, and the New International Bible—footnote the words "Red Sea" to read "Reed Sea" or "Sea of Papyrus."

Understand that until the scholarly world began to cast doubt on the true location of the Red Sea, the Bitter Lakes of the northern Sinai were *never* called the Sea of Reeds. They were simply bitter lakes. But since reeds can't grow in salt water— and by extension of the Red Sea—early translators targeted the lakes as a ready fresh-water option for a place where reeds might grow. But if the Bitter Lakes were in fact the Red Sea of the Exodus, what do we make of 1 Kings 9:26? That text speaks of how "King Solomon also built ships at Ezion Geber, which is near Elath in Edom, on the shore of the Red Sea." If this Red Sea were the Bitter Lakes, Solomon must have assembled his entire fleet of ships in the middle of the Sinai desert—impossible at the time. Solomon's port at Elath is located on the Gulf of Aqaba. And the Gulf of Aqaba forms the eastern arm of the Red Sea.

In his self-published book, *Search for Pharaoh's Chariots*, Knuteson explains the riddle as a simple case of misplaced vowels. The words *Yam Suph* can also read *Yam Soph*. And *Yam Soph*, as the New King James Bible contends, is translated "Sea at land's end." *Sea at land's end!* That's it! We're talking about a body of water bisected at the southernmost tip of the Sinai Peninsula, precisely where our search for Pharaoh's chariots culminated. This translation fits the biblical scenario perfectly. The Red Sea crossing is, indeed, at *the sea at land's end.*

HOW LONG WERE THEY GONE?

"The LORD, the God of the Hebrews, has met with us. Let us take a three-day journey into the desert to offer sacrifices to the LORD our God" (Exod. 3:18).

We come now to the second prong of this two-part intrigue, the one that throws most off the scent of the true route of the Exodus: How long did it take the Israelites to reach the Red Sea? The question goes hand in hand with the proximity of the Red Sea crossing point. And make no mistake about it—correctly answer these questions and you can accurately retrace the Exodus route.

"Let us take a three-day journey into the desert."

To this day, many scholars underscore the Bitter Lakes theories by citing this scriptural reference to a three-day journey. Recall the story: when Moses returns from exile, he asks Pharaoh for three days in which the Israelites might journey into the wilderness to worship God. It's here that most take a wrong turn. Three days correspond loosely with the approximate walking time from Goshen to the Bitter Lakes. Some believe that once Pharaoh expelled the Hebrews from Goshen, they walked three days into the desert and encountered the Egyptian army at the edge of the Sea of Reeds, where God parted the waters and ushered the Israelites to safety. In that way everything can be located in the Sinai Peninsula. The pieces seem to fit.

Yet on closer scrutiny the theory falls apart.

Early in the Book of Exodus, we read how Pharaoh angrily denies Moses' request for three days' leave of absence. His rebuke sets the stage for a devastating cycle of plagues: hail, locusts, frogs, fleas, boils. God turns the Nile to blood, and then, in a final assault, strikes dead the firstborn throughout Egypt (Exod. 12:12). Pharaoh's own son dies in the Passover terror. Torn between horror and vengeance, he kicks the Jews out of Egypt, crying: "Up! Leave my people, you and the Israelites! Go, worship the LORD as you have requested. Take your flocks and herds, as you have said, and go" (Exod. 12:31–32).

Is it reasonable to assume that, reeling from such a nightmare, Pharaoh's officials expected the Israelites to go three days into the desert, worship God, then return? Did the Jews take three days, or was the trip much longer? Would Pharaoh, his country decimated by plagues, have been able (or even disposed) to respond within a three-day window? Does it make sense that Moses and company, fleeing Egypt after four hundred years in slavery, would stop three days into their journey, only to wait for the Egyptian chariots to swoop down? Common sense says no!

So does Scripture. Nowhere in the Bible are we told the Hebrews traveled three days anywhere. Rather, the text suggests it took Pharaoh at least twice that long even to begin assembling a militia. Remember, Egypt was a country in crisis. Terror gripped Pharaoh. Scripture says,

"Egypt was glad when they left,
because dread of Isreal had fallen on them"
(Ps. 105:38).

So the Hebrews took their leave of Egypt, a company of "six hundred thousand men on foot, besides women and children" (Exod. 12:37)—easily an army in excess of two million people. Even subtracting their "large droves of livestock, both flocks and herds," they could not have moved quickly (v. 38). At some point "Pharaoh and his officials changed their minds and said, 'What have we done? We have let the Israelites go and have lost their services!' So he had his chariot made ready and took his army with him" (Exod. 14:5–6). (Another reason, by the way, to disregard the "three days' journey" theory. Pharaoh clearly thought the Hebrews were gone forever, not for a mere three days.)

How long did it take Pharaoh to respond? Scripture is mute on the subject. Yet using even conservative numbers, it figures the Israelites were gone a minimum of four days before Pharaoh's advisors suspected they weren't coming back. Let's assume Pharaoh sprang to action the moment he found out. Such a call to arms, with primitive means of communication, must have taken another week to muster troops from as far away as four hundred miles, thus enlarging the Hebrews' head start to over a week. All the while, Scripture says, the Israelites traveled at a brisk pace, day and night (Exod. 13:21).

No matter how you calculate it, God's children had a head start of some consequence—a lead that could take them many days beyond Goshen and well past the Bitter Lakes. It could easily have taken them to a point somewhere on the Red Sea coast, for even as Pharaoh's troops hotly pursued them, the Israelites kept "marching out boldly" (Exod. 14:8). The Hebrews had ample time to travel the approximately 170 miles down the western Sinai coast, curve around the southern tip of the peninsula, and find themselves trapped at the "sea at land's end." Here, at the Straits of Tiran, Knuteson believes, the Israelites first saw the dust of Pharaoh's chariots.

So why have most commentators turned a blind eye to this possibility? We can't say for sure, but it's fair to speculate. To many minds, the uncut Exodus account presents several dilemmas. For one, how could a massive body of water be parted down the middle? By the hand of God? It's easier for many to believe that a good, stiff breeze blew in from the Mediterranean at just the right instant, and with enough force, to part the shallow Bitter Lakes.

But how would such a scenario give great "glory" to God, as Scripture insists it did? Three times in Exodus 14:17, God says he split the Red Sea to "gain glory for himself." Again in Exodus 9:16, he says he divided the sea to show "my power and that my name might be proclaimed in all the earth." Psalm 106:8 says God did it "to make his mighty power known."

Some power—a little snort of wind to dry up temporarily an inconsequential bog. Big deal.

Unless, of course, it didn't happen that way at all. What if it took place just as a simple reading of the account suggests? What if God really did lead his chosen people out of Egypt by pillars of cloud and fire, then stand guard as Moses stretched his hand over the sea, "and all that night the LORD drove the sea back with a strong east wind and turned it into dry land. The waters were divided, and the Israelites went through the sea on dry ground, with a wall of water on their right and on their left" (Exod. 14:21–22)?

I believe it happened just as the Bible says. As we'll soon see, evidence for these events makes the Bible look mighty good.

185
Λ

Twenty

LORD OF THE NORTH

After inspecting the Bitter Lakes, the second stage of our mission called for us to survey the rugged Sinai interior for viable routes to the Red Sea. Even after dismantling the "Reed Sea" thesis, dozens of theories remained. Most concerned obscure paths and oblique desert byways.

Some theoreticians say the Israelites drifted north or south of the Bitter Lakes, then took a northern track, camping at any of a handful of Mount Sinai prospects in the upper peninsula's Desert of Shur. Others insist they deployed due south from Goshen, tracking on the west side of the Gulf of Suez (dodging the Bitter Lakes altogether), and crossed into the peninsula from the west branch of the Red Sea. Still others insist that, after passing through the Sea of Reeds, they dropped south, cut due east across the desert, and cut a swath through the foothills to Jebel Musa.

On a map, all appear feasible. But we wanted to inspect the actual turf, to see what the terrain itself had to say. Driving inland from the Bitter Lakes, the impossibility of most of these theories quickly became apparent. Away from the coastline, the topography seems virtually impassable. Any of the aforementioned routes through the peninsula would have stranded the Israelites in extremely rugged mountain terrain or trapped them in bottlenecks of gorges pinched closed by twisting ravines and blind cul-de-sacs. These constricted byways would have crippled the Exodus escape, ensuring the doom of the throng already slowed by children, the aged, and enormous herds and flocks.

So which routes remained? What circuit through the wilderness did God choose to lead his children to the sea? Here again, Scripture speaks clearly. Consider Exodus 13:17–18: "When Pharaoh let the people go, God did not lead them on the road through the Philistine country, though that was shorter. For God said, 'If they face war, they might change their minds and return to Egypt.' So God led the people around by the desert road toward the Red Sea. The Israelites went up out of Egypt armed for battle."

Clue number one: *God did not lead them on the road through the Philistine country, though that was shorter.* Aside from the impossible terrain found on the inland routes, in the Sinai interior the Hebrews would likely have met up with hostile Philistine tribes—an eventuality God apparently foresaw and wanted to avoid, knowing his skittish flock might turn back.

Clue number two: *God led the people around by the desert road.* What does "around by the desert road" (v. 18) imply? Scripture

says God led his people by pillars of cloud and fire, around by
the desert road to the sea. Where might such a road be found?
The verse suggests a roundabout route, skirting the Sinai interior and avoiding the Philistines. The only logical match is the
western Sinai coastline.

Sure enough, we found this coastal region to form a natural
roadway "around" the tip of the peninsula to the eastern
branch of the Red Sea. It's a roomy ribbon of seaboard that
would have furnished the Israelites an easy-access passage, wide
enough for an army of two million to march in a broad column.
Today, this westward advance sports a modern roadway all the
way from Goshen to the southern tip at Sharm El-Sheik.

We followed this desert road around the horn of the peninsula
to the Gulf of Aqaba, where it stops dead at the Straits of Tiran.
The coastline comes to a dramatic (and completely unexpected) end at the base of an imposing mountain range, whose
tall, sheer peaks jut almost vertically from the shoreline. This
fascinating rock barrier presents a natural obstruction that
abruptly halts further travel up the coast. What's more, it cor-
responds almost perfectly to the blockade implied by Scripture
that thwarted the Hebrews' forward progress at the edge of the
Red Sea: "Then the LORD said to Moses, 'Tell the Israelites to
turn back and encamp near Pi Hahiroth, between Migdol and
the sea. They are to encamp by the sea, directly opposite Baal
Zephon. Pharaoh will think, "The Israelites are wandering
around the land in confusion, hemmed in by the desert" ' "
(Exod. 14:1–3). Note especially the phrase "Baal Zaphon" (or
"lord of the north").

Was this towering rock actually Baal Zaphon? Does the phrase, "lord of the north," refer to this peculiar mountain range running down the edge of the sea, forming an impregnable wall where the Hebrews found themselves "hemmed in"? Seeing it firsthand made it seem as though the Bible were spoon-feeding us clues to a treasure map. We had taken the desert road around the horn and found ourselves hemmed in by the wilderness and the sea. Unable to proceed up the coast, we were forced to "turn back," just like the Israelites.

It seemed as though we had arrived at the historic crossroads—the same climactic junction of land and sea—that caused Moses to stop and Pharaoh to think, *The Israelites are wandering around the land in confusion, hemmed in by the desert.* The lump in my throat told me we had found the true route to the Red Sea.

IN—OR OUT—OF EGYPT?

A fellow in combat fatigues waved our bus to the side with his machine gun—another U.N. checkpoint, one of a handful we passed on our southward tour of the Sinai coast. The checkpoints came out of the Six Days War, a peacekeeping presence monitoring traffic in and out of Egypt. A threat of terrorist activity still festered throughout the Sinai interior. For us the checkpoints presented little more than a nuisance, prying us from our air-conditioned bus and depositing us into the withering desert.

At noon we grabbed lunch and stretched our legs. As I stepped from the bus, I instantly felt the pavement broiling the soles of my boots. Each breath I took of this fire-baked wilderness burned the inside of my nostrils. I thought it the most God-forsaken place on earth, an evil, alkaline blotch unfit for human occupation. The desert seemed to stretch forever into scalding emptiness.

Then, from the horizon, I saw a tiny black speck inching toward us. At first I couldn't make it out, but minutes later I could see it was a camel, with a man on top, bobbing over the dunes. Colors slowly emerged, until finally I realized I was witnessing an ornately arrayed man and camel decked out in gold tassels, bronze bells, sparkling sequins, and jangling batons, dancing madly in the sun. Just as we finished our lunches, this bouncing whirlwind dismounted in a billow of dust.

The man's flowing robe unfurled like an Egyptian flag as he slid off the beast. The handler approached us with a toothy smile and the breathless spiel of a carnival barker: "*Camel rides . . . five do-llars! Please, gentlemen, I am at your service!*"

I laughed out loud. This was the last place I expected to find a pushy vendor trying to fleece the tourists. My amazement grew when two guys from our team happily forked over five bucks and took the camel for a spin around the bus. I couldn't stop grinning. What a strange, bewildering land—equal parts mystery and buffoonery.

As we waited to clear the checkpoint, Knuteson challenged us with yet another question: "Was the Sinai Peninsula, at the time of the Exodus, under Egyptian control? Was it part of the Egyptian empire?" If it were, he wondered, why would the Israelites spend forty years wandering here under Pharaoh's nose? Knuteson then explained that Egypt's ancient boundaries held sweeping consequences for our search. The matter cut to the heart of the Exodus controversy and the true location of

Mount Sinai. Why, if the Hebrews fled Egypt under a death sentence, would they tarry in the land of their blood enemy?

It's another grave difficulty for those who endorse the "traditional" view of events, that is, the "Sea of Reeds" crossing point and the peak at St. Catherine's. Those folks would have us believe the entire forty-year wilderness saga unfolded inside the Sinai Peninsula, under Egypt's watchful eye (or at least within its jurisdiction). The problem is often reconciled by positing the Sinai Peninsula as part of *Arabia* in those days, not Egypt at all.

Such a solution, of course, would fit what we've already seen: Galatians 4:25 says Mount Sinai sits in *Arabia*. If the peninsula were indeed part of Arabia during the Exodus, the Israelites could have wandered undetected for a time in what amounts to Egypt's backyard. This much is certain: Moses never would have stayed in a land occupied by Egyptian military and economic forces. So if the Sinai were under Arabian rule back then, it would at least help to justify the notion that Mount Sinai sits near St. Catherine's.

The problem is, the Sinai Peninsula *was not* in Arabia but Egypt. Egypt's borders were roughly the same then as now. A medley of historical sources concur: Egypt's borders haven't changed appreciably from the time of Pharaoh. *Smith's Bible Dictionary*, for one, describes Egypt as "a country occupying the northeastern angle of Africa," whose limits appear "always to have been nearly the same." Smith cites Ezekiel 29:10 (and 30:6) to assert: "The whole country [of Egypt] is spoken of as extending from Migdol to Syene—or roughly the same southern and eastern limits we find today."

Ancient records show the southern Sinai Peninsula was buzzing with Egyptian copper and turquoise mines from approximately 5500 to 1150 B.C.[1] If the peak at St. Catherine's were legitimate, it would mean the holy mountain of the Jews sat squarely in the middle of Egypt's busy commercial zone. (From Scripture we know the Exodus occurred in approximately 1446 B.C., well within the time of Egypt's large-scale mining interests and accompanying security force.)

Petroglyphs near St. Catherine's Monastery depict hundreds of workers mining turquoise. Turquoise artifacts that could only have come from the southern Sinai have been found in ancient Egyptian tombs.[2] In his book *Desert of Exodus*, H. Palmer pinpoints the southern Sinai as a hotbed of Egypt's royal mines. He concludes that the Israelites would never have migrated in that direction for fear of the Egyptian army, camped year-round near the minefields.[3] This copper and turquoise trade (Egypt's primary currency in Moses' day) linked Cairo with oceangoing merchants on the Red Sea. All this points back to one overriding fact: the Sinai Peninsula has *always* been an important part of Egypt.

Can there be any doubt that Moses and the Israelites put as much distance as possible between themselves and the Egyptians of the Sinai Peninsula? In this area bustling with Egyptian holdings, settlements, and troops, two million Hebrews would have blanketed the countryside. Any attempt to travel undetected in such a constricted area for even a day— much less forty years—would have proven impossible. And consider this: Scripture tells us that not once in forty years did the Israelites come in contact with Pharaoh's forces.

The idea that Israel marched circles in the Sinai desert after the Red Sea miracle, then pitched a leisurely camp at Jebel Musa, is preposterous. It rails against reason. Loitering anywhere near the peak tourists now revere as Mount Sinai would have assured their destruction. It was, to us, as clear as the platinum Sinai sky. Still, we had to see the mountain for ourselves.

Twenty-One

EGYPTIAN IMPOSTOR?

So this was what it was like to freeze to death. Lying on my brittle, frigid cot, I suspected I had entered the latter stages of hypothermia. Hoping to generate a little body heat, I took every stitch of clothes from my suitcase—T-shirts, underwear, dirty towels, socks—even newspapers and open books, and covered myself from head to toe. But the only thing that did was make me feel totally ridiculous.

Outside, snow fell as howling winds blew icy gusts through gaps in the window frame. I tried to caulk the holes with toilet paper, but the snow kept whipping in on top of me. My room felt colder than a meat locker. I had long abandoned any hope of a restful night's sleep; all I wanted now was to survive till morning with all my toes.

Appearances to the contrary, this wasn't a frozen Gulag in Siberia but my motel at St. Catherine's Monastery, located two miles from

Jebel Musa—in *Egypt*. I'd been misled! I understood this was to be a hot excursion into steaming deserts and balmy gulf-stream beaches—places not normally associated with down parkas. All I had was a light cotton sweater, hardly equal to the freezing temperatures biting us here at St. Catherine's, five thousand feet above sea level.

When our team arrived, we discovered all the respectable inns lining hotel row were booked solid. We were left to fend for ourselves with leftovers. The crew scattered, and I found myself lugging my bags down the road and over the tracks to a row of stone huts on the outskirts of town—the village's overflow quarters, a former shepherd's hostel steeply overpriced at two dollars a night.

As the night wore on, I listened to a drunken band of heavily armed Egyptian soldiers singing Arabic dirges twenty paces from my door. They broke bottles and fired rifles into the air beside a blazing fire pit. I imagined them singing songs about killing all the American capitalist pigs. *Which will come first*, I wondered: *will I freeze to death or get dragged off by this gang of inebriated goons?* I envisioned myself blindfolded, standing before a firing squad, loose underwear and socks dangling from my shivering body—a frozen mummy from the Goodwill shop. At another burst of gunfire, I slid from beneath my shroud and propped an old plastic chair against the door. I knew it wouldn't stop a flea, but at least I'd hear it fall if someone broke in. I wouldn't go down without a fight!

As snow collected in drifts on the floor, I tried to conjure an illusion of warmth. I imagined myself as Peter O'Toole as Lawrence of Arabia, guzzling water in the desert to stay alive.

Suddenly the door burst open, the plastic chair rattling across the floor. There stood a stunningly beautiful woman, her big, almond eyes sparkling in the dim light of a bulb hanging near the door frame. She had long auburn hair, a dainty nose, and high cheekbones. I lay still under my layer of laundry, trying to decide if I were dreaming or if I'd already frozen and gone to heaven. In both her hands she carried bulky suitcases. Her eyes darted about the room. She stepped cautiously closer and saw me grinning idiotically from the shadows. Then this vision of loveliness gave me a look of such disgust as to turn flesh to stone and spouted, "*You're* not Henry! What room number is this?" She turned in a huff, slamming the door behind her and shuffling her bags to the next hutch. Through the wall I could hear her scream: "Hen-*rry*! If you *ever* again drag me to some God-forsaken place in the dead of winter to see Moses' mountain . . . *I'll divorce you!*"

I lay my freezing head back on a dirty, bunched-up towel, closed my eyes, and prayed for morning.

A MUSTY SURPRISE

I awoke to see Jebel Musa awash in a brilliant morning sun. *I had survived. Hallelujah!* My fingertips and toes might be numb, but somehow I had avoided frostbite.

The daylight sadly disclosed the full scope of the tourist trap that had grown up about the monastery. A dingy row of roadside shanties offered all manner of Mount Sinai trinkets, candy, and religious mementos. One turbaned chap used an old whiskey bottle to roll out flat-bread cakes on a fifty-gallon drum he'd cut in half and propped over an open fire. The tasteless, impoverished commercialism jolted me from the reverent mood I had summoned for the occasion.

Early that morning a monk ushered us quietly to the monastery's basement, a dark and musty catacomb smelling of the rot of fourteen centuries. He led us into dense shadows that opened into a huge room, divided in the middle by a chicken-wire facade. There, behind the wire mesh, sat a formless mass, cluttered and fuzzy in the murky backdrop. "Walk over here," said the elderly monk, motioning us on. "You must see it up close."

198

We pressed in close to the wire, and in the flash it took for my eyes to adjust, I imagined a cache of old Bedouin swords and spear points stored from centuries past or crown jewels from the ancient turquoise and copper mines that once riddled these uplands. Then I heard Jim Irwin gasp. I turned to see his flinty jaw go slack. I jerked around to squint hard into the shadows, and as the pall lifted, I saw we were looking at a knobby mountain of human skeletons—hundreds of them. It stole my breath. Was this a killing field? Had the monastery been an extermination camp? No one spoke for several seconds.

Finally the monk grinned. "Please, don't be concerned," he said. "These are the bones of the monks who have died here at St. Catherine's Monastery since it was built. When a monk dies, he is buried in our courtyard cemetery. Because space is limited, we dig up the body three years later and put the bones in here." Words escaped us, so he calmly proceeded, "It's our tradition. The bones are a constant symbol of our temporal existence, reminding us daily of our insignificance here at the foot of Mount Sinai. We all know our bones will one day be thrown in that pile with the others. It helps us keep our eyes off ourselves and on God."

It made strange sense to me. Staring at the rack of skulls stacked to the rafter like apples in a cellar, I understood how the practice would foster a chastened spirit. In the middle of the pack lay a skeleton of some prominence, propped in a high-backed potentate's chair and attired in a moth-eaten velvet robe. *One of the monastery's founding abbots,* I surmised. Of the hundreds of skeletons in that room, each had no doubt belonged to a devout man of God. All had served here believing that this monastery stood astride holy ground, near the mount where Moses met with God. The monk led us back upstairs into the sunlight, where Jebel Musa, the mountain they called Sinai, towered in the distance.

I'm told the skeleton room isn't part of the standard tour; someone in our party had made a special request. The official tour ends upstairs on the back church wall, where tourists stop and gawk at a scrawny vine. They say it's the actual burning bush of Mount Sinai, where God told Moses, "Take off your sandals, for the place where you are standing is holy ground" (Exod. 3:5). Judging from the cloud of tourists genuflecting and crossing themselves, and getting their pictures taken next to it, many believe the claim. I couldn't help noticing those who slyly plucked its leaves and stuffed them in a purse or pocket. How had the poor thing survived so long?

The Emperor Justinian built this "Monastery of the Burning Bush" in 536 A.D. to protect newly arriving monastic orders from harassing nomadic tribes. It was later renamed St. Catherine's Monastery in honor of the saint said to have been beheaded for challenging Roman Emperor Maximinus about his persecution of Christians. Today, her name is the one most widely associated with Mount Sinai. Millions worldwide have made the pilgrimage to southern Sinai to pay homage here. It is a hallowed site whose reputation is best reflected by the monks who call it home. Asked why he chose to live and work at this remote and lonely outpost, one young monk solemnly replied, "It's the most holy place on earth. It's where God walked."

WE'LL SEE FOR OURSELVES

After a late breakfast Jim Irwin and I set off to climb the mountain, agreeing to keep open minds about what we were about to see. Following a trail of old stone steps laid by the monks, we hiked to the peak's summit, willing to be convinced that Jebel Musa was indeed Mount Sinai. By the halfway point of our two-mile climb (the mountain rises to a height of approximately 7,500 feet), already we were duly unimpressed. It seemed just a mountain.

Nothing we saw excited much interest, certainly nothing to inspire the bubbly enthusiasm registered by the explorer E. G. Robinson in 1838, the first time he saw Jebel Musa: "It was a scene of solemn grandeur, wholly unexpected, and such as we have never seen, and the associations which at the moment rushed upon our minds were almost overwhelming."[1]

My first response? Huge disappointment. Down below we could see the tour buses and curio stands and hear noisy Bedouins bartering with tourists for camel rides to the top. From where we stood, it seemed little more than a seedy tourist trap. Nothing about the mountain distinguished it from other mountains in the region. Silently, I began asking myself, "Who *says* this is Mount Sinai?"

As I later learned, a fourth-century fortune teller said it first: Queen Helena, mother of King Constantine and a mystic of some renown, designated Jebel Musa as the real Mount Sinai following a "prophetic vision." (Later she claimed to identify the location of the Holy Sepulcher in Jerusalem, Jesus' birthplace in Bethlehem, and the plot of ground where the cross of Christ was supposedly buried.) The problem is, Jebel Musa was never verified as the real Mount Sinai by legitimate scholarship. The mountain upon which we now stood was declared to be so by nothing more substantial than Helena's royal proclamation.

As we climbed those stone steps, we paused often to examine an odd crevasse or jutting knoll but saw nothing of biblical note. On top sat a little monastery built in the sixth century by Emperor Justinian, a perfect vantage from which to admire the riveting vistas and the adjacent peaks and valleys. I found it breathtaking, but Jim seemed oblivious to the scenery. Like a skilled diamond cutter, he studiously appraised the finer facets of the landscape. I'd seen this hyper-intense attention to detail before, on our trips to Mount Ararat in Turkey. It's what made Jim a great astronaut. Now in full explorer mode, he tossed out rhetorical questions, made copious notes, and sketched the scene. With Bible in hand he asked, "If this is Mount Sinai, where would all the people have camped? Where are the altars? The pillars? Where are the streambeds?" At the time all I knew about Mount Sinai was the Ten Commandments and the movie by Cecil B. DeMille. So I took my lead from Jim.

201

∧

At the summit we left the trail and hiked across the mountain face, assiduously examining its every crag and outcropping, scouting its hidden walls and gullies from top to bottom. We looked for specific features: geologic obelisks, peculiar terrain, or man-made imprints that would harmonize with the biblical narrative. What did the Bible say Mount Sinai and its surroundings should look like?

For starters, Scripture tells of a broad battleground close to the mountain, big enough to host Israel's epic contest against the Amalekites: the valley beneath the "top of the hill" where Aaron and Hur held Moses' arms aloft as the battle raged below (Exod. 17:10). But at this mountain we found no sign of any battleground, anywhere.

Scripture also describes a plain around the mountain large enough to accommodate two million campers—an immense campground by any measure. A commanding view of the lowlands showed us Jebel Musa's perch high in a rugged mountain range, an impossibly steep pitch for an expansive campsite. Two branches of wadis meandered between nearby mountain ranges, but these narrow ravines could have harbored but a small fraction of the enormous assembly. The "traditional campsite" noted by scholars cannot even be *seen* from the top of the peak—this in spite of Exodus 19:2, which confirms the Hebrew campsite lay immediately adjacent to the mountain. The Israelites "camped there in the desert *in front of* the mountain." But from our vantage Jebel Musa had no front to speak of.

Another verse says God instructed Moses to "put limits for the people around the mountain" (Exod. 19:12) so that curious onlookers wouldn't go near it or touch it. God forbade even the animals from approaching: "Not even the flocks and herds may graze in front of the mountain" (Exod. 34:3). The *real* Mount Sinai had to be girdled about by spacious fields and meadows for flocks and herds to graze; but Jebel Musa has no place for flocks.

Let's recap. Directly in front of the real Mount Sinai must be a sweeping, broad expanse; Jebel Musa has nothing resembling an adjoining plain or desert where two million campers could pitch a tent. It has no pastures for massive flocks and herds and no vast valley or spacious battleground—all shortcomings that should long ago have exposed it as a pretender.

We kept looking anyway, rounding the mountain and searching the valley floor for other critical features. Did it boast a large mountain stream—either on or near the peak—that might have satisfied the immense water needs of a parched multitude? No. We found only a cramped and rocky, high-desert dust bowl, utterly bereft of water. What's more, we saw no indications or prehistoric signs of flowing water—no ancient riverbeds, springs, or creek bottoms, no telltale signs of the torrents described in Psalm 105:41:

> "He opened the rock, and water gushed out;
> like a river it flowed in the desert."

We came across no water-polished stones or boulders left behind from ancient river bottoms, creeks, or lakes; no depressions or pits suggesting reservoirs or other water-storage facilities.

Finally, we tried to determine whether such an assembly could even have fit in the surrounding lowlands. Subtracting by half the most reliable population estimates of the Hebrew assembly (approximately two million men, women, and children), we determined that the surface area of the valley floor would have allowed less than one square yard per person—a ludicrously small tract, unfit for a gargantuan tent city and its grazing herds. Neither could we locate a logical staging area for the people to construct, and later worship, at the altar of the golden calf (Num. 10:3). Nor was there a site anywhere near the mountain where the "Tent of Meeting" could have set (Exod. 38:8). The rugged, congested ramparts about Jebel Musa fit none of these criteria.

Our search nonetheless lasted until dusk as we feverishly sought traces of ruins, carved chips, or rubble from altars or pillars, stone markers, even evidence of burning activity—God was said, after all, to have descended on the peak like a furnace of fire (Exod. 19:18). As an investigative detective I was an expert in gathering evidence, and I can tell you we looked for *anything* to give this traditional site the benefit of a doubt. Yet on every front it failed decisively. Its lowlands could not have hosted the vast base camp of the Exodus. We saw none of the biblical fingerprints that should have been apparent, no clear evidence of God's handiwork, no physical basis to suggest it was the sacred ground from which a holy nation sprang.

By the time we reached the bottom of the mountain, camel drivers still vied for clients, vendors still hawked their garish trinkets from squalid stands. The overpowering stench of animal and human waste filled our nostrils. "This is ridiculous," Jim said irritably. "There's no *way* this is Mount Sinai."

I gazed ambivalently at the peak. Then I remembered to whom I was talking—the first astronaut to explore both the Hadley Rille and Apennine Mountains of the *moon*. Jim Irwin was not only a master navigator, expert surveyor, and trained scientist; he was a world-class explorer, a modern-day Marco Polo. The lunar module pilot for Apollo 15 was telling me, with set jaw, "Bob, this ain't it!"

I knew then that despite what the Egyptian Department of Tourism will forever insist, the peak at St. Catherine's is a cheap knockoff. The Exodus multitudes had not camped at Jebel Musa. The true Mountain of God *must* be elsewhere. With that settled in our minds, we hurried back to the hotel, gathered our bags, and hopped on a bus bound for the Straits of Tiran.

205

Twenty-Two

THE ROAD IN THE DEPTHS

After St. Catherine's Monastery we made a beeline for the gulf, eager to complete our mission. Our findings at the Bitter Lakes, the Sinai coast, and, finally, at Jebel Musa, convinced us we were on the right track. We followed a trail that led us to the "sea at land's end" on the western branch of the Red Sea, just as Knuteson and Dick Ewing had predicted. Everything was in place—the yacht, our detection equipment, the divers— but suddenly our quest for Pharaoh's chariots stalled.

From the day of our arrival, we had been targeted by the Egyptian Coast Guard, clearly hostile to the presence of an Israeli archeologist we'd invited, on an American expedition, and on board an American-flagged ship. It began as a series of untimely intrusions over apparent "technical problems" with permits and visas and such, then escalated into full-scale harassment. It came to a head on day four, when the coast guard boarded our yacht at gunpoint, searched, and shut us down until everyone's passports and permits could be reviewed. They sent us ashore as they ransacked the boat, interrogated us, and rifled through our papers—a maddening waste of time.

Still, after wintry Jebel Musa, it felt good to be back at sea level. A generous, consoling sun warmed our backs the morning Jim and I strolled out to the edge of the Red Sea. Ironically, we languished ashore at almost the exact spot on the beach where Roy Knuteson believed the Israelites had crossed the Red Sea.

With some time to kill, Jim and I figured we'd inspect the shoreline for telltale signs of the crossing. Since we stood close to the mountain barrier we understood to be "Baal Zaphon," where the Hebrews probably came to a sudden dead end between the desert and the sea, it seemed plausible that something from that climactic episode had survived. No doubt someone among the million-plus terrified Hebrews had discarded some possessions—pottery, tools, weapons, utensils, jewels—as they ran for their lives into a towering canyon of water. Maybe some of it still lay buried under the beach, waiting to be found.

We borrowed the expensive Garret Electronics Metal Detector the divers would use to scan the sea floor for metallic particles. At the edge of the beach, a little old Bedouin man met us, face frowning with worry. He pointed to a sign written in Arabic and clearly wanted to tell us something. But since he couldn't speak English, we nodded politely and kept walking. The lovely beach, covered in fine white, ashtray sand, yielded small reminders of the Six Days War—primarily the half-buried, rusted implements of military hardware.

Egypt had blockaded these key shipping lanes in 1967, cutting off Israel's economic lifeline and making official its intent to "wipe Israel off the map." Its action brought centuries of hatred and hostility to a violent head.

But Israel proved no pushover. Quick to retaliate, Israel launched a devastating air attack that flattened Egypt's air force before it could leave the tarmac, as well as an armored tank blitz that routed the armies of both Jordan and Syria at their southern borders. The military masterstroke won Israel possession of the Sinai Peninsula and a short-lived buffer from her sworn enemies. Israel returned the peninsula to Egypt in 1973, ushering in a season of uneasy truce. Throughout the peninsula, however, the wares of that bloody campaign remain much in evidence.

I didn't care. The war had ended; the sea looked beautiful. I was happy to be strolling the beach in bare feet, letting the warmth soak into my bones. Waving the metal detector aimlessly over the sand, I daydreamed of snorkeling in the gulf's pristine waters. Suddenly I noticed something from the corner of my eye—an odd-looking hole, or pit, sitting in the middle of the beach, about twenty paces from shore. Walking closer, I saw a crater, fifteen-feet in diameter, scorched and blackened around the rim.

Hmmm. Bizarre, I thought. Then I saw what looked to be discarded scraps of a ratty brown rug tossed in the bottom of the hole. Inching closer for a look, I stopped dead in my tracks. This was no rug! I was looking at the shattered remains of a camel, its rotting folds, splintered hide, and sun-bleached bones peeking through the sand.

I glanced back and saw the old Bedouin poking his head from behind a rock and waving his arms frantically in the universal sign language for: "*Get out of there!*"

We had strayed into an abandoned mine field!

210

Bombs left from the war riddled the beach; the poor camel had wandered in and been blown to bits. Trying to keep my wits, I turned to Jim and said, in my calmest voice, "Houston, I think we have a problem." Jim turned to see the crater, the mangled camel . . . and was struck mute. Too scared to move, he finally forced a grin and pointed to the metal detector, making a slow, sweeping motion with his arms. Then, with mock confidence, he barked an order: "Houston, get us out of here."

I hastily obliged. Using the metal detector as a makeshift minesweeper, we gingerly worked our way backward, retracing our steps to safety. Soon we stood on asphalt, staring at each other in disbelief. After a giddy pause, we began laughing uncontrollably. Even the Bedouin laughed, graciously accepting our thanks, yet shaking his head in bewilderment as he left us to our reckless ways. Still chuckling nervously, I handed Jim the metal detector and turned for one final look at the shoreline.

And . . . *there it was!*

THE HIDDEN REEF

It snaked through the water like a giant, ghostly hologram: the mysterious, underwater land bridge we had waited to see this whole trip. We knew it was here, somewhere. It had shown up on NASA satellite imagery Dick Ewing had obtained prior to our departure: a thin, spectral sliver of ghost-white reef stretching almost across the straits to Saudi Arabia. And here it was, right off the beach, jutting seaward at approximately the spot Knuteson and Ewing calculated the Red Sea crossing must have occurred. Late in the day, it looked like a brooding behemoth shimmering in the surf, its serpentine shadows bathed in the rays of a crimson sunset. I turned to tell Jim, but he had already started walking back to the motel. When I looked back, it was gone, lost in the glare of high tide.

"Your path led through the sea, your way through the mighty waters, though your footprints were not seen" (Ps. 77:19).

The next day, after customs finally released our papers, we undertook a thorough reconnaissance of the underwater reef. We charted its location, verified its dimensions, and measured its depth below the water line. The satellite images had, indeed, revealed a jumbo jet-sized runway of unclear composition, coiling barely visible beneath the surface. At the time we weren't certain what we were looking at, but later it became a key reference point, signaling where to anchor and muster our efforts to find Pharaoh's chariots.

The reef angled perpendicular to the shoreline, forming a wide passageway that rose from the depths like a barnacle-backed blue whale. The prophet Isaiah had spoken cryptically of just such a "road" in the depths of the sea:

> "Was it not you who dried up the sea,
> the waters of the great deep,
> who made a road in the depths of the sea
> so that the redeemed might cross over?"
> (Isa. 51:10).

The team's excitement level soared; any minute we expected to see ancient chariots bobbing in the surf.

At last, a key physical link to support our Exodus theories and address doubts that have dogged scholars for centuries. With the discovery of the underwater land bridge, pointed questions about the Red Sea crossing could now be framed. Who would've guessed? A veritable highway in the depths, ushering the Hebrews to safety.

Later that night, sitting aboard the *Fantasea*, adrenaline pulsed through my veins; I was living the dream of every adventure junkie. Touring ancient lands, sailing the Red Sea, finding physical evidence of one of the Bible's definitive miracles. It was the stuff of fairy tales. All indifference washed away in this flood tide of discovery.

Still I was perplexed. Due north sat an oddity out of *Ripley's Believe It or Not*: a five-hundred-yard-wide coral reef, invisible on the surface yet spanning the entire straits like a stealth aircraft carrier. How could it be? My eyes had seen it, yet was this *really* the "road in the depths" immortalized by Isaiah? Was it the byway God made so "the redeemed might cross over"?

The other theories had proved a mirage—the Bitter Lakes deceit, the hoax at St. Catherine's. But this land bridge—what a find! Even thousands of years after the Exodus, eroded and battered by the sea, it remained a sturdy underpass, wide and firm enough to support an armored tank division. To this point in the journey, I had quietly yielded to the group's consensus. As I followed along step by step, it all made sense. But seeing this wondrous reef bowled me over. It appealed to so much more than my intellect; it engaged my heart. For the first time I remember feeling as if maybe *it all really happened!*

THE ARGUMENTS

When one takes a moment to ponder it, a natural, underwater land bridge in the Straits of Tiran makes perfect sense. Even disregarding God's awesome act of deliverance—

> "By the blast of your nostrils
> the waters piled up.
> The surging waters stood firm like a wall;
> the deep waters congealed in the heart of the sea"
> (Exod. 15:8)

—this invisible reef gives a wholly practical explanation for how the crossing was achieved.

The Red Sea boasts banks so steep that, even if it somehow miraculously dried up, its very depth would pose an insurmountable obstacle. Without some sort of landing or viaduct—or *road*—to bridge the gulf, "crossing the sea" would mean descending into a steep canyon, then climbing back up a drastic incline to reach the other side. Today the waters in the straits reach a maximum depth of about seven hundred feet (though the waters have undoubtedly receded over the millennia); yet along nearly every other mile of coast the sea floor plunges to excessive depths, with great cliffs dropping off as much as three thousand feet. At these depths, fording such a chasm would be akin to marshaling the inhabitants of a major U.S. city deep into the Grand Canyon, without a clear-cut trail, and herding it back up a near-perpendicular cliff wall—all in a short time. But at the Straits of Tiran, the underwater land bridge, impeccably positioned at one of the shallowest points on the gulf, eliminates that logistical nightmare. And satellite imagery has confirmed no other land bridge exists on either gulf of the Red Sea.

The Bible also says the Hebrew assembly crossed over on dry land: "And the Israelites went through the sea on *dry ground*, with a wall of water on their right and on their left" (Exod. 14:22, emphasis added). By "dry," we assume Scripture means *dry*. Yet the sea bottom here would have been anything *but* dry in the wake of the receding waters. Geological surveys verify most of the Red Sea floor is covered in mud forty to sixty feet deep, a feature that probably hasn't changed much over time. An ebbing torrent like that described in Scripture would have rendered the sea bottom an impassable slough of thick, loose mud, leaving the Hebrews to navigate a veritable plain of quicksand. Such conditions would hardly abet a swift flight to safety!

The coral reef we inspected is sturdy and broad enough—and situated in water shallow enough—to meet this "dry land" criteria. Two million Israelites, columns of cattle, flocks, fleets of carts and wagons—even Egyptian troops and chariots—would have been able to pass quickly over the tightly compacted coral without getting their feet wet.

Finally, Scripture reports that the entire Israelite nation crossed the expanse by the "last watch of the night" (Exod. 14:24), indicating a total walking time of no more than five to six hours. Only at the Straits of Tiran would a quick nighttime crossing have been possible. The distance from shore to shore along both branches of the Red Sea averages from ten to twenty miles, translating into a minimum of two to four days walking time. The distance shore to shore at the Straits of Tiran, however, is no more than two miles—by far the narrowest channel on both sides of the gulf. It seems God providentially provided a walking bridge at the only point on the gulf where a multitude could cross in a single night!

This stretch of reef stands as one of the most remarkable finds of our Egyptian adventure. It embodies, like nothing save Mount Sinai itself, an astonishing convergence of geologic and oceanographic anomalies; and it exists at just the right place to confirm the biblical record and liberate the Israelites from the Sinai Peninsula.

Finding this land bridge tightened the scope of our exploration for the chariots and incited an insatiable itch to find the real Mount Sinai. The hidden reef became a giant compass arrow pointing due east, to the Arabian side of the gulf. Our search for the chariots faltered, but in my heart the adventure had just begun. I'd seen Isaiah's "road in the depths"—an arrow lodged deep in the flank of Saudi Arabia.

Twenty-Three

LETTER OF DESTINY

The last night of our stay in Egypt, our team enjoyed a festive debriefing on the deck of the *Fantasea*. It had been an arduous two weeks. Everyone was primed to unwind, say their good-byes, have a few laughs, and trade war stories about an eventful enterprise. There would be no earthshaking discovery of chariot wheels on this trip (though Ewing and Knuteson both vowed to return with even more sophisticated equipment, more time and resources, and try again). Nonetheless, a mood of elation prevailed. We took great satisfaction in knowing we'd helped draw a new line in the sand concerning the Exodus route. If nothing else, we'd proven to ourselves that the Bitter Lakes were not the Red Sea crossing point, nor Jebel Musa the real Mount Sinai. And with the remarkable discovery of the underwater land bridge, we'd found as stirring and practical an explanation for both the Red Sea crossing point and the location of the real Mount Sinai as any theory to date. Bidding one another good-bye, we shared a quiet belief that the real Mount Sinai remained a mystery yet to be solved.

It was exciting fare, worthy of a spirited adieu. As the evening wore on, Jim Irwin pulled Larry and me aside to a quiet corner of the yacht. Reaching in his shirt pocket, he showed us a crumpled letter he received shortly before the trip from a fellow named David Fasold. The note detailed a journey Fasold and a fellow named Ron Wyatt had taken into Saudi Arabia some years earlier, where they evidently found and scouted a peak called Jabal al Lawz. To hear him describe it, the mountain possessed all the distinctive earmarks of the real Mount Sinai.

Reading from the letter, Jim described features on the mountain that, if nothing else, indicated Fasold had found something incredibly interesting. Unfortunately, as he left the mountain, Fasold was arrested by Saudi police and spent a terrifying week in jail, charged by the king's prosecutor with "robbing Saudi Arabia of its wealth from antiquity," a capital offense. Fasold was finally released, though badly shaken and stripped of his film, video, notes—all the evidence needed to authenticate his find. He'd risked his life and come up empty, though the harsh Saudi response suggested he'd found an archaeological site of some sensitivity and significance.

Fasold told Irwin he wouldn't return—it was too dangerous. He'd written the High Flight Foundation in hopes an astronaut of Irwin's stature might have the clout to gain official Saudi clearance to mount a legitimate excavation of the peak. In sum, his letter stated: "Here is a fascinating place. Its features make us believe it is Mount Sinai, but we don't have anything to prove it. All my photographs, maps, notebooks, etc. were confiscated by the Saudi military. The mountain is called Jabal al Lawz. It sits in the middle of a military reservation, fenced in by chain link and barbed wire." Fasold had given it a heroic try; now he wanted to pass the torch to someone else who might be able to get in (and out) with the goods.

After what we had just been through, the letter lent stunning force to Knuteson's theory: practically everything we'd seen on the trip advanced the notion of Mount Sinai in Saudi Arabia. Dangling the letter between thumb and forefinger, Jim smiled and raised his hand toward the eastern horizon. There, out-lined by a vague line of mist scarcely visible in the twilight, lay the eastern Saudi shoreline.

"What did I tell you, fellas?" Jim said, voice edgy with expectancy. "*That's* where we need to go." Jim handed the let-ter to Larry, who tucked it carefully in his shirt.

How this information affected me, I didn't yet know. But from that moment my mind began to echo with a single question: *What's at the other side of the land bridge?* I felt a sense of urgency and suspense—perhaps something like what Jim felt before his moon shot—of what it would be to find a religious site of such historic magnitude.

We spoke no more of it that night. But as we returned to the party, my eyes caught Larry's. In his deadpan expression, I thought I caught the faintest glint of acknowledgment, that kindred spark of wonder, needed to launch two incurable thrill seekers into the cherished unknown.

We were going. And we'd find the mountain, one way or another. Of that we were sure.

EPILOGUE

A COMET BLAZING ACROSS THE HEART

In the years since my search for Mount Sinai,
I've been interviewed by everyone from cub
reporters to national TV talk-show hosts, most
of them curious about how an ordinary guy like
myself, rather than a trained theologian,
scholar, or archaeologist, found the crown jewel
of the great Exodus. Explaining that I simply
trusted the Bible to lead me to the mountain, I
can often see a flash of agitation in their eyes,
followed by the testy follow-up: *Why should I
care about Mount Sinai?* It's a valid question, one
that I enjoy answering.

The answer lies hidden in the query itself. As
overwhelming response to my story illustrates,
people from all walks of life *do* care deeply
about Mount Sinai. But like the talk-show
hosts, they can't always put their finger on *why*.

As time passes and I learn more about this
amazing monument, the more astonished I am
by its visceral power to disrupt the staid thinking of brilliant theologians and hardened

skeptics. And I am constantly humbled by its capacity to invigorate the faith of beleaguered believers. Certainly a mountain on whose craggy slopes the seeds of modern civilization were planted gains quick access into the imagination. Why else would thousands of tourists flock to St. Catherine's Monastery in the southern Sinai Peninsula? Why do scientists and believers debate the origins of the Shroud of Turin? Why do millions of Christians trek to Jerusalem for expensive tours of the Holy Land? Why, indeed, do archaeologists spend careers digging around for ancient biblical relics?

Why? *Because people want to touch history.* They want to see and walk where the prophets walked, stand where Jesus preached and prayed, and, if they're fortunate, to touch the hem of his robe. Above all, they want to believe. They visit Egypt hoping to pay homage to the land where Moses sojourned, to take in the views, project themselves into the mystery of the great Exodus. They want to take home a piece of Mount Sinai, where God reached down with his own finger and wrote the Ten Commandments.

Believers have a compelling, unspoken need to see and touch these famous landmarks. It stirs in them a fresh appreciation of their spiritual heritage, reconnects them with the physical roots of their faith, lets them relive a bygone era. It builds faith at a time in history when science, academics, philosophy—even the laws that govern us—seem to be trying to dismantle the biblical worldview and neuter God. Amid this onslaught believers search for something, anything, to corroborate their faith; something tangible they can hold and say, "Look, world, I'm not crazy. And *here's the evidence!*"

So we circle back to the question: Why should I care about Mount Sinai? In ways other shrines and landmarks cannot, Mount Sinai, because it speaks so eloquently to the authenticity of God's Word, undergirds both faith and biblical doctrine. Its very existence brings a vital energy to the realm of apologetics. In our travels through the Middle East and into Saudi Arabia, we found the Bible to be a fiercely accurate, almost connect-the-dots map to the holiest sites of classic Judaism. In the end God's Word was all we needed to find God's holy mountain—a peak both captivating and inspiring.

The swirl of interest surrounding Mount Sinai reminds me of the hubbub attending the release of the movie *The Prince of Egypt*, the top-grossing animated feature based on the life of Moses. The media fanfare and public response to this movie help explain the mystery and intrigue of Mount Sinai, for, as any rookie media consultant will agree, what Hollywood produces these days carefully mirrors the cultural zeitgeist: the spirit of the age, what a society is interested in, thinking about, consuming.

Response to *The Prince of Egypt* shocked social critics who questioned why, in 1998, a major studio would spend $70 million on a feature based on the Old Testament and (some would say) its timeworn rehash of the Exodus story. For many, it bordered on scandalous that Moses still enjoyed star quality in Tinsel Town.

The media hummed with cranky anecdotes about the film's religious and historic overtones; everyone from *Time* to the local tabloid questioned whether Moses was an actual person or merely overblown legend. The undisguised cynicism bleeding through most of the commentaries intrigued me. One article in the *Denver Rocky Mountain News* framed itself around a single question: Did Moses really exist? The writer queried a panel of Bible critics, historians, even Christian pastors, and concluded that evidence of Moses' life doesn't satisfy modern standards of proof. "There are no contemporaneous written documents to back up the stories that, as far as can be determined, were written down 200 to 500 years after the time in which Moses would have existed," the panel declared. [1]

One expert flatly asserted, "The historical evidence of Moses is insufficient." Another conservative Old Testament professor added, "We don't have the type of corroboration historians use to write history." I was surprised to hear a theologian at a prominent southern theological seminary make such a comment, but it soon became clear that even staunch Christians bow to the prevailing bias. The most startling quote came from a Hebrew historian in Cincinnati who said, "There is no historical evidence of Moses . . . *outside the Bible.*"

Don't get me wrong. I'm no scholar. I understand the narrow criteria by which judgments based on "modern standards of historical evidence" are made. Yet I marvel that such comments pass without a shrug. The implications seem painfully clear: the Bible in itself is not a reliable historical document. Holy Scripture, upon whose words and principles the spiritual beliefs and inspiration of millions of Christians rest, doesn't pass muster in the halls of academe. God's Word is not to be trusted as a voice of perspective in the global marketplace. It certainly doesn't prove Moses lived.

224

So we are left to conclude that Moses probably didn't exist. He is instead reduced to an allegorical symbol of early Israel's need for a mythic hero, or of man's search for meaning, or some such nonsense. Sadly, the growing weight of opinion casts a resounding vote against the authority of Scripture. Taken a step further, it's a silent ballot against the God of the Bible.

It's little wonder we find ourselves in such a predicament. The fact is, to date we have no physical evidence of the miracles God performed throughout Scripture. We have no photos of the Red Sea splitting, no footage of pillars of cloud and fire, no petrified footprints where God walked with Abraham. At the traditional site of Mount Sinai in Egypt, we are left with nothing to indicate God's enduring presence—no scorched peak, no split rocks or ancient riverbed, no cave of Elijah, no ghostly stone pillars or hand-cut shrines—in fact, no trace whatever of the great Exodus or what might have resulted from God's extraordinary penmanship of the Ten Commandments.

As at other "holy" tourist sites in the Middle East, one leaves St. Catherine's with a heightened sense of history, perhaps an imagination stirred toward the heavenlies—but little else, certainly nothing with which to declare to the world, "Look here! Hard evidence of the God of my faith! Here, look—his unmistakable fingerprints!"

Which brings us back to the significance of the *real* Mount Sinai. What would it mean if someone found it—actually found and brought to light the mountain spoken of in the Bible? Might a peak blackened and superscorched at its crest serve as a convincing fingerprint of an all-powerful Force descending "on it in fire," making solid rock smolder and billow "like smoke from a furnace" (Exod. 19:18)? Might ancient fire pits and stone markers, maybe even massive altars and a series of features uncannily mirroring the peak's biblical resume, strike some as evidence of a climactic gathering point, perhaps of the great Exodus? How would it affect modern sensibilities? How would reputable voices react to physical evidence of these extraordinary events?

What would it mean to spiritual seekers to behold a religious site of such significance, rising from the pages of Scripture like a granite behemoth, appearing just as Scripture says it *should* look, located precisely where Scripture says it *should* be? Would it help restore confidence in the credibility of God's Word? Would scholars look at the Bible differently, or at least credit it with some historical value? More importantly, would seeing the graphic remains of God's handiwork energize and fortify the faith of millions of dispirited Christians?

That night on the Gulf of Aqaba, when I felt the call to undertake a legitimate search for the real Mount Sinai, it was raw adventure I sought. I relished the thought of a dangerous mission in a foreign land. It filled me with anticipation, the kind I imagined Jim Irwin felt as he prepared to land on the moon. But that ultimately faded in the face of larger questions. Something else gripped my heart, a sense that, somehow, this obscure monument held answers to issues I wrestled with. From my earliest thoughts of Mount Sinai came whisperings of religion, hints of eternity, pangs of convictions I once held as a child. Sure, it promised rugged thrills and high adventure, maybe even some glory. But I waded unwittingly into much deeper waters. Mount Sinai came to define my own messy search for significance.

THE ENORMITY OF GOD'S PRESENCE

What other monument or religious icon rivals Mount Sinai's storied stature? Where else did God engage man in a fashion so intimate, yet so awesome and overpowering, that many prominent theologians seem uncomfortable acknowledging it ever existed? The enormity of God's influence at the site takes one's breath away. With the obvious exception of the cross of Jesus, more public miracles of God's mighty intercession in the lives of men took place at Mount Sinai than at any other place, or time, in history.

227
Λ

They include that surreal moment when God first spoke to Moses at the burning bush: "Moses! Moses! . . . Take off your sandals, for the place where you are standing is holy ground" (Exod. 3:4–5); and the place where the Lord declared himself for future generations: "I am the God of your father, the God of Abraham, the God of Isaac and the God of Jacob" (Exod. 3:6).

The Lord chose Mount Sinai from among the earth's great pinnacles, setting it apart in a pointed directive to Moses: "When you have brought the people out of Egypt, you will worship God on this mountain" (Exod. 3:12). It was the site of one of the Old Testament's transcendent moments, when God showed Moses his glory. "There is a place near me where you may stand on a rock. When my glory passes by, I will put you in a cleft in the rock and cover you with my hand until I have passed by" (Exod. 33:21–22). Here God stood before Moses at the rock at Horeb and slaked the thirst of the parched Israelites, instructing Moses to strike the rock so that "water will come out of it for the people to drink" (Exod. 17:6).

Later, at the foot of the mountain, Moses met daily with God at the Tent of Meeting. God appeared in a pillar of cloud (Exod. 33:10), and Moses spoke with him face to face, retiring from those encounters with his own face shining like molten silver (Exod. 34:35). And while the Israelites were camped there, Moses received instructions to build the ark of the covenant, where God's presence dwelt through subsequent generations (Exod. 25:10–22). The ark was built from acacia groves on the mountain's hillsides.

228

Finally, and most important of all, Mount Sinai is the fabled birthplace of the Ten Commandments. On that peak God delivered the code that formed the cornerstone of Mosaic society, a system of law and order that has governed every civilized society since. These commandments remain a remarkable canon whose historic and spiritual significance cannot be overstated. They were the result of God's consummate gesture to a people he chose to separate for himself, setting in motion for all time (and in the most dramatic way possible) his absolute standard of human conduct. Defying laws of nature as we understand them, he reached down and, with his own hand, inscribed the commandments on stone tablets. The method and magnitude of this singular act stagger the imagination.

Phil DelRe, a pastor and Ten Commandments scholar, contends that "the true interpretation and practical application of the Ten Commandments is the greatest kept secret in hell. Its value and significance to mankind cannot be overstated— neither can the relevance of the absolute standard of right and wrong written on the heart of every man from the beginning of time to the end of the world. The Ten Commandments are the standard God is going to use when every man stands before God to give an account of his life." DelRe adds: "The Ten Commandments are the heart of the Bible; the rest of the Bible is simply a commentary on the Ten Commandments. Mount Sinai is where God chose to hand down this divine document to humankind."[2]

As the arena, then, for some of God's greatest works, the implications of Mount Sinai loom enormous, awe inspiring. As no other natural landmark can, the mountain brings hard focus to mystifying truths. It is a stone sentinel calling us back to God at a critical moment in time. For like the Israelites thirty-five hundred years ago, who stood at a distance, gaping as God descended on Mount Sinai in smoke and fire, we too must shake off the chains of our captivity. Though freshly liberated from four hundred years of slavery, the Israelites had about them a stench of worldliness, polluted by Egypt's pagan influences. But on Mount Sinai God began the cleansing process. There he ministered to them day and night. They were his people, and at the mountain his healing glory remained ever before them.

Today, who would question there is a stench about God's people? We have been enslaved in a modern-day Egypt, informed in our attitudes and corrupted in our actions by worldly ideals. We have been persuaded by pagan gods of television, sex, fame, and success. The culture's priorities have become our priorities.

Mount Sinai illuminates Scripture like nothing else. It turns our gaze to God as a comet blazing across the night—for it sometimes takes fireworks to get us to look heavenward, to shift our attention from the mundane to the divine. Mount Sinai locks

the human mind back on God and on his Word. For this reason, this mountain is either one of the unique archaeological
coincidences in all history, or it is where God stepped out of
eternity to reveal himself as never before or since. If it is the
real Mount Sinai, it is one of the most stirring discoveries of all
time.

> Has anything so great as this ever happened, or has
> anything like it ever been heard of? Has any other
> people heard the voice of God speaking out of fire, as
> you have, and lived? Has any god ever tried to take for
> himself one nation out of another nation, by testings,
> by miraculous signs and wonders, by war, by a mighty
> hand and an outstretched arm, or by great and awe-
> some deeds, like all the things the LORD your God did
> for you in Egypt before your very eyes?

> You were shown these things so that you might know
> that the LORD is God; besides him there is no other.
> From heaven he made you hear his voice to discipline
> you. On earth he showed you his great fire, and you
> heard his words from out of the fire. Because he loved
> your forefathers and chose their descendants after
> them, he brought you out of Egypt by his Presence and
> his great strength, to drive out before you nations
> greater and stronger than you and to bring you into
> their land to give it to you for your inheritance, as it is
> today.

> Acknowledge and take to heart this day that the LORD
> is God in heaven above and on the earth below.

> —Deuteronomy 4:32b–39

ΠΟΤΕS

Chapter 18, "The Bible Says It's So!"

1. Itzhaq Beit-Arieh, "Fifteen Years in Sinai—Israeli Archaeologists Discover a New World" *Biblical Archaeological Review* 10 (1984): 52.

Chapter 19, "Charmed in Goshen"

1. See Nelson Glueck, *Annual of the American School of Oriental Research* 15: 1–3; see also , W. F. Albright, *Bulletin of the American School of Oriental Research* 109: 15.

Chapter 10, "Secrets of Al-Bad"

1. Frank Moore Cross, *From Epic to Canon* (Baltimore: Johns Hopkins University Press, 1998), 66.

2. Richard N. Ostling, *Sun Herald* [Southern Mississippi], "Lead up to Pope's Visit, Mount Sinai's Time, Whereabouts in Question," February 19, 2000, D3.

Chapter 18

1. *Biblical Archaeology Review* (July 1984), 52.

Chapter 20, "Lord of the North"

1. W. M. F. Petrie, *Researchers in Sinai* (London: Murray, 1906).

2. Ibid.

3. E. H. Palmer, *Desert of Exodus* (New York: Harper, 1872).

Chapter 21, "Egyptian Impostor?"

1. Edward G. Robinson, *Biblical Researches in Palestine, Mount Sinai and Arabia Patraea* (London, 1938), 91; Roy Knuteson, *Search for Pharoh's Chariots* (Fort Collins, Colo.: self-published, 1990), 82.

Epilogue, "A Comet Blazing Across the Heart"

1. *Rocky Mountain News* article cited by Wayne Lee Gray, *Fort Worth Star-Telegram* (December 31, 1998), 4D.

2. Author's interview of Phil DelRe, February 16, 1998. DelRe is found of Voice in the Wilderness Ministries, Des Plaines, Ill.